M000290367

THE
CROSS
IN
THE
CULTURE:
CONNECTING OUR
STORIES TO THE
GREATEST STORY
EVER TOLD

RUTH **BUCHANAN**

The Cross in the Culture

© 2020 by Ruth Buchanan

All rights reserved. No part of this book may be reproduced in any form by any electronic or mechanical means including photocopying, recording, or information storage and retrieval without permission in writing from the author except in the case of brief quotations embodied in critical articles or reviews. Unless otherwise indicated, Scripture quotations are from the ESV® Bible (The Holy Bible, English Standard Version®), copyright © 2001 by Crossway, a publishing ministry of Good News Publishers. Used by permission. All rights reserved.

Scripture quotations marked KJV are taken from the King James Version. Emphasis to Scripture has been added by the author.

Cover design and interior formatting by TK Consulting & Design, LLC.

Author photo © 2016 by Rita DeCassia Photography
Published by Build a Better Us

For Hilary and Laura,
who came along for the ride.

The Cross in the Culture
Table of Contents

Introduction

When we say *culture*, we're often referring to the social institutions and achievements of a particular nation, people, or other social groups. But *culture* can also refer to "the arts and other manifestations of human intellectual achievement regarded collectively."[1] When we use the word *culture* in this book, we will be thinking less about how people behave socially and more about how they express themselves creatively—specifically, in their stories.

Society's cultural artifacts speak to who we have been in the past, how we see ourselves now, and who we want to become in the future. Needless to say, society's answers to these questions do not always align with ours. Because of this dissonance, Christians raised on a wave of "culture war" ideology may not know quite what to do with their love of culture. For a long time, I felt similarly conflicted.[2]

In these pages, we will seek not to war against the culture but to steward our cultural gifts well, recognizing all the ways in which they point toward the presence of our Creator. We will journey together through storytelling genres, tracing our Savior's steps all the way. And make no mistake: he is there. Sometimes his presence is overt.

---

[1] *Oxford Languages*, s.v. "Culture," https://www.lexico.com/en/definition/culture (accessed June 4, 2020).
[2] Though they are nowhere quoted in this book, two specific works have greatly influenced my thoughts on Christian cultural engagement. I commend to you *Culture Care: Reconnecting with Beauty for Our Common Life* by Makoto Fujimura and *Culture Making: Recovering our Creative Calling* by Andy Crouch.

Sometimes it's covert. Either way, once we know how to look, we will find him everywhere.

We seek Christ in our culture by pursuing his pathways through our stories—the ones we tell one another and the ones we live in real-time.

Ruth Buchanan

PART I

Chapter 1

|

There was a time when, if you had told me you could see the cross of Jesus Christ reflected in the culture, I wouldn't have understood what you were talking about even if you gave me specific examples. It's not that I didn't understand the cross. I didn't understand the culture.

To recognize the cross in the culture, you must view this world for what it is, understand your place in it as a Christian, and see yourself as both a product of society and a contributor to it. You must understand not only the gospel's personal implications but also its collective ones. God is not just in the business of redeeming you—he's demonstrating his glory by redeeming his Bride and restoring the entire cosmos. Faith is not just a personal matter, and God doesn't just work through Christians. I mean, he spoke through a donkey once. That should be all the evidence we need that the Redeemed aren't the sole reflections of his majesty and glory.

I didn't always see things this way, though. Let me start by telling you a little bit about where I come from. I wasn't brought up in the culture, and though I'm an American Christian, I wasn't raised in the Evangelical bubble. Not exactly.

I want to be clear. My family was not in a cult. We weren't members of a commune or a collective. I wasn't raised in a bunker like Kimmy Schmidt. Yet when I started my first job, I was just as clueless about what my coworkers were talking about most of the time. Sometimes I still feel like a recovering mole woman.

This is both a weakness and a great strength.

Not Exactly the Bubble

When I talk to siblings in Christ who came to faith as adults, they sometimes mention experiencing culture shock when they joined a Christian community. When I talk to believers raised in Evangelical backgrounds, they'll describe having grown up in bubble. Neither situation describes me perfectly, and yet I've experienced both sides. Though I grew up in a Christian home, my family wasn't part of America's Evangelical subculture. We weren't in the bubble. In a bubble, you can see what's going on in society but not interact with it yourself. What we experienced was more like a rabbit burrow.

Let me explain.

Rabbits burrow underground. There, they create nests and systems of tunnels. Rabbits who live in the same area will often link their systems together, resulting in a little underground complex all its own. That's how I grew up. Safe and protected, but definitely separated. Lots of freedom to run around—but all in a closed system.

When I was born in the late 1970s, my family was living in rural Pennsylvania. Though I was technically born in Lancaster (known for its Amish and Mennonite communities), I spent my childhood in nearby Lebanon County. Back then, it was all rolling pastureland, farms, and cows. Once when an old tree in a field was cut down, it made the paper. It was that kind of place.

We lived in a township. If you're not familiar with American rural life, townships are smaller even than boroughs. They're generally so sparsely populated that public services are either done by volunteers or handled by the county or state itself. Our community had its own police force, but there were only two officers. They traded off shifts and took turns with the one car. They only patrolled on weekends.

We weren't a farming family, but to live in this part of Pennsylvania was to be at least partially integrated into the lifestyle. If you didn't live on a farm, your friends did; and if you hung around, you helped do chores. You wore Levi's and owned a pocketknife and climbed trees and jumped in cow pies. You rolled down grassy hills in summer and sledded down them in winter.

Our little house abutted a cornfield. We kids considered it an extension of our backyard. To this day, that field haunts me. When movies show someone running through a field in terror, slapping cornstalks as the music pounds, my chest constricts. Running through a cornfield is just as scary as it looks, even if all you're running from is your older brother. To be fair to Nathan, it wasn't hard to scare me in those days, especially in a field. Any random noise could be the combine harvester, chewing its way through the rows to gobble me up.

My terror of the harvester was not misplaced. They absolutely kill people. Rural life is full of dangers, and people in the country tend to hurt themselves in ways that become stories later. Machinery goes awry. Big animals are unpredictable. Everyone has axes and rifles. Neighborhood kids goad you into unwise risks. More than once, I was talked into touching an electric fence. (Yes, more than once.)

My parents, who were transplants to that community, remained outsiders during our nine-year stay. They'd grown up elsewhere, weren't related to anyone nearby, and had college educations—which our neighbors believed ruined your good sense. Though these distinctions made it hard for them to fit in, they allowed my parents to offer us kids broader worldviews.

We were educated about life beyond our community—though not too far beyond. My parents couldn't take us down roads they hadn't yet traveled themselves. Dad was from a western Pennsylvania railroad town, and Mom had grown up in a Scandinavian pocket of Illinois. She hadn't even tried a taco until she was in her twenties. She'd simply never seen one before.

They did their best to broaden our horizons, but it was hard. In our township, there were no museums, theaters, or cultural centers. There was a library, but it was so small, it was actually inside a house.[3] Going to the library was a weekly outing year-round. I carry vivid

---

[3] This wasn't a public library in someone's home. It was a dedicated public building in a former residence—a small brick house in a residential area. I just looked it up on the internet, and this little library is still functioning. Same place, same red-brick façade, still going strong thirty years later. They've updated the inside and put an addition on the back, but everything else looks frozen in time. I'm now feeling incredibly nostalgic and may go have a little cry.

memories of running my hand up the polished wood of the spiral staircase whenever we arrived to re-check out our favorites from the tiny collection. We were allowed to read whatever we wanted, as often as we wanted. Remember, in the rabbit warren there is freedom within a closed system. Reading is an area in which I've always felt free.

We also subscribed to *National Geographic* magazine, and my siblings would fight over new installments the way kids fight over screen time. I'd curl up sideways in a favorite chair, ogling two-page photo spreads. Women from Myanmar, their necks stretched by coiled silver rings. Didn't that hurt? What would happen if they took them off? Then there were the Beijing cyclists queuing by dozens at a traffic light in the rain. I took my time, staring at each face in the sea of brightly colored rain ponchos. Where were all those people going? What were they thinking? Imagine riding bicycles in the rain with that many people around. I couldn't picture that many people in one place, let alone riding bicycles together.

At that point, I couldn't imagine even being in a city. But big changes were already on my horizon. I just didn't know it yet.

The Move

In 1988, our family moved to Florida. The announcement came as a shock. Dad was going to switch from being a small-town pastor to being a suburban church planter. As I understood at the time, this meant being the pastor of a church that didn't exist.

Florida in the late '80s was something else. I've heard stories about the drug culture back then, particularly in Miami, but we were moving to the suburbs. At that time, our section of South Florida was still a sprawling, underdeveloped patchwork. We lived in a city laid out by planners but still largely uninhabited. The roads were paved, but they were graced by very few actual houses. In my neighborhood, empty lots loomed between the widely spaced concrete block homes.

As children accustomed to spending all unschooled hours outside, we quickly learned that spare lots were the only places with shade enough to keep us from boiling alive. Overgrown with scrub pine, cabbage palms, and Brazilian pepper plants, they were satisfactory substitutes for the cornfields. Less scary but with their own unique dangers. You only have to step on a sand burr once. We traded bare feet for flip-flops and learned to adjust.

Adjusting socially was another matter. We'd just come from a rural township—a tiny, deep-rooted farming community where everybody knew everybody and were most likely related. Now, we lived in a suburb full of transplants from other states.[4] Major roads were still only two lanes, and grass grew upward through cracks in the streets. However, with chain retail stores now within driving distance from our house, we felt more a part of real-time American life.

I missed the country. Our township had not been densely populated either, but there we had lived as members of a community—

---

[4] I didn't meet my first true Floridian for years.

not fully integrated, mind you, but we had friends and were accepted. In Florida, it was different. Kids didn't meet up outside to jump in cow pies, climb trees, slide down hills, run around the corn field, and ride bikes all afternoon. It was simply too hot. They visited friends' houses to swim in screened-in backyard pools or play inside under the cool blast of the air conditioner. Making friends under such circumstances wasn't so simple, especially if you've just moved to Florida and only know one other family.

The School

When we lived in Pennsylvania, homeschooling didn't feel isolating. Our social lives were rounded out with church friends, community sports leagues, and endless outdoor play with neighbor kids. It was different in Florida. Especially in the early days after the move, we lacked a strong social network. Since our city was still underdeveloped, school options were slim. So was the family budget. Our parents settled on sending us to a small Christian school in a neighboring city.

Though I wouldn't have recognized this distinction at the time, the ministry operating this school was a part of the Independent Fundamental Baptist movement (IFB). I met some great friends there, had a few good teachers, and have actually stayed in touch with some of them. On the whole, however, the Fundamentalist schooling experience was overwhelming and confusing. When I say it was overwhelming, I don't mean from an academic perspective. If anything, the work was easier than what we'd been doing at home. I mean it was overwhelming for social and spiritual reasons. Up to that point, we'd lived fairly sheltered homeschool lives, but this was on another level.

At school, they taught us that women should wear skirts—only and always. If women absolutely had to do anything active, they should wear bulky split skirts dubbed *culottes*, a voluminous, pleated affair that bore little resemblance to what the fashion industry labels *culottes* today. I will never forget participating in P.E. outside in the Florida sun while wearing a polo shirt and pleated, double-knit culottes.

Men's clothing standards were fairly normal, but their hair could be only just so. Television was of the devil, and going to a movie theater was a terrible sin. Bible verses, which we memorized for most classes in addition to subject-specific coursework, were to be studied in the King James Version only. Other English translations were not considered real Bibles.

In those days, I had a mint green Precious Moments Bible I simply adored—not so much for the dewy illustrations but for the fact that once I'd gotten it, I started underlining every single verse I'd read.[5] I've always been big on tracking achievement, and it was important to me that I keep my underlining system current. That way I would know when I finally finished reading the entire Bible for the first time. But I couldn't take my Precious Moments Bible to school—it was the New

---

[5] I just looked this Bible up, and there is a copy for sale on Etsy. It was produced in 1985 and is marked *vintage.* I think I need a nap.

International Version. As a workaround, I would write down whatever verses we read at school in my little planner and do the underlining later once I got home. It was exhausting.

My parents encouraged us to respect our teachers at school and not argue with them, even the areas in which we clearly disagreed. That was tough because sometimes our teachers openly criticized the types of things our family did at home. My natural response is to speak up and question, but neither the environment nor my parents' instructions allowed me to do that. Mostly I just stewed and fretted. The upshot of all this was a lot of unnecessary spiritual angst.

My parents weren't totally hands-off when it came to the school and its rules. Occasionally, they would intervene. Once my mother spent an afternoon in the principal's office defending my brother's hair. He'd recently gotten a fresh cut, and though it did not violate any of the explicit rules, it had still been judged "too worldly." My suspicion is that he simply looked too much like Vanilla Ice for comfort, with or without the notched eyebrow. Mom took the rule book in and asked them to show her how Nathan's hair violated the rules. I don't remember what the verdict was, but I remember being really proud of her. To my eyes, strolling into the principal's office to leverage the rules in your own favor was such a power move, especially impressive coming from my phlegmatic mother.

While there were limits on how far my parents would take their hands-off approach to the school's standards, it wasn't always clear to me as a child where those lines were. So much of the legalism drilled into us at school didn't match what was being taught about Christianity in our home and church, yet it all purportedly came from the Bible.

Lost in the Fundamentals

From Fundamentalism, I learned to fear the culture. Visiting evangelists who preached in chapels constantly railed against the dangers of movie theaters, popular music, "Christian rock," and mainstream TV. They taught that listening to rock and roll would cause us to have premarital sex.[6] That by consuming society's coded messages through movies, music, and TV, our lives would spiral into rebellion, alcoholism, drug abuse, and early death.

A major emphasis was on dressing the "right way" and not doing the "really bad" sins—swearing, drinking, dancing, listening to music with syncopated rhythms, having sex, or associating with anyone who did those things. At home and in our small church, however, we learned that a righteous life came as God changed our hearts, helping us love him and love our neighbors. When our hearts were changed, we began to develop the fruit of the spirit, which would lead to changed behavior and transformed lives.

---

[6] Once, a middle-aged evangelist explained to us in chapel that rock and roll got its name because listening to it causes your body to want to mimic the physical actions of sex—rocking and rolling. As a pretty naïve seventh grader, I didn't understand what he was talking about. I mean, I knew the concept of sex but not the physics involved. I asked a friend on the bus to explain the evangelist's comments. I'm still scandalized that an adult male would talk to children like this.

Though not Fundamentalists themselves, my parents were what I'd call Fundamentalist-adjacent. Especially while they were raising us. We weren't in line with all the standards held by our Fundamentalist school, but we were toeing it. Though they didn't consider the King James the only inspired version for the English-speaking people like my teachers did, we did use the KJV at home and in church. My soul is still drenched with this language.

We owned a TV, but for much of our time at home, it wasn't kept in a main room. We had to go down to the unfinished basement or out on the back porch to watch it. Mostly, we watched the news and some sports. We occasionally watched cartoons and classic TV our grandpa taped and sent to us on VHS in the mail. When I say I've seen endless episodes of the original *Lost in Space* series, I mean they were *literally endless*. Grandpa would forget he was taping and cut away to a Braves' game.

Lots of things our friends did, we weren't allowed to do. We didn't go trick-or-treating. We didn't go to movie theaters, listen to contemporary music (whether secular or Christian), or keep up with any pop culture. For a while, we weren't allowed to have playing cards in the house.

Here's where we return to my rabbit warren analogy. Between a sheltered home life and a Fundamentalist school, I was pretty out of the loop socially. If you don't consume pop culture, especially living in a time before the internet, you really have no idea what's going on outside your nest. Again, this is both a strength and a weakness.

When I say I knew nothing about what was going on in the world, I mean it. We didn't even watch *Sesame Street*. Once, when a neighborhood friend and I ran into her house to grab a cold drink from the kitchen, I spotted an interesting magnet on her fridge. It was plastic and shaped like a spangly silver glove.

Me: What's that?

Her: That's Michael Jackson's glove.

Me: Who's Michael Jackson?

Her: WHO'S MICHAEL JACKSON?

Me: I'm asking you.

I was a child coming of age in the 1980s who didn't know who Michael Jackson was. To this day, I'm still asking who people from my childhood are. The difference now is that I'm used to the strange looks.

I'm not here to complain. My childhood was safe, warm, happy, and loving. Our parents protected us, connected with us, and taught us useful skills. They raised us to be caring and compassionate. We ate well, slept well, played hard, learned to love the Creator, and avoided much that is harmful and scary. Barring the odd moment when kids would gaze at me as if I'd recently docked on earth, I didn't know what I was missing. In the long run, you could make a case that I wasn't missing much that truly mattered.

But here's the thing. I didn't realize how out of sync with my peers I was. How ill-equipped I would be to talk to people who weren't already like-minded. How fundamentally shallow my understanding was of their lives and problems. How poorly prepared I would be to contextualize Christian belief for people who didn't already know what I was talking about. It was like we were living in separate timelines, concurrent but totally parallel. The complications didn't present themselves for a while.

Reading Between the Lines

The fact that I could engage society through print is what made the biggest difference for me. The whole world opened up through books.

Truly, we were allowed to read whatever books we wanted. I even read *Flowers in the Attic,* V.C. Andrews's salacious 1979 novel about abused (and incestuous) siblings. To be fair to my parents, they didn't know I was reading it and would not have approved if they had. That's the thing, though. I don't remember my parents ever restricting access to anything at the library, checking up on what we were reading, or worrying about what we were absorbing through print.

In that respect, they were much more permissive than the parents of my ultra-conservative friends, who worried about what unsanctioned books could potentially expose their children to—and I'm not just talking about sexual content. They worried about what opposing viewpoints would do to their children's spiritual formation. My parents didn't seem to fear that opposing viewpoints would corrupt us; and as a result, we didn't fear it, either. Instead, we were taught to filter everything we were reading through the lens of truth and ask questions about anything we found odd, strange, or confusing.[7]

In many ways, learning to live in that tension was an education all its own. This dynamic profoundly shaped my emotional, spiritual, and intellectual development—though it could be tough relationally. Soon, I knew more than my peers—yet still, somehow, so much less.

Life in the Warren

This is what I mean when I said I grew up in a rabbit warren. In a bubble, you see what society is up to—you are just limited in how you can interact with it. In the warren, however, I could run around with a seeming sense of freedom, safe and protected, yet having little clue what's taking place above my head.

Acquainting myself with Evangelicalism over the last few decades, I've experienced my share of culture shock. Our touchstones are so different. In my corner of Christianity, we weren't listening to big-name speakers, attending conferences, or going to the rallies and concerts. I once had my Walkman taken away because I'd been listening to DC Talk.[8]

"You got in trouble for listening to *Christian music?*"

---

[7] I never asked any questions about *Flowers in the Attic*. Though, clearly, I had them. I still do. So many questions.

[8] *Free at Last* on cassette, borrowed from a friend.

17

Reader, I did.

Church Life

Church hits different when it meets in your living room.

Once we moved to Florida, our church plant initially met in our home. We started with eleven people—six of them our immediate family. We eventually outgrew the living room, but not by much. We stayed very small for a long time, meeting for years in a rented warehouse. I have intense memories from this period of my life, the majority positive. We saw God save souls, form a close-knit spiritual community, and provide for us in miraculous ways. I still live out faith lessons God taught through those experiences.

During those years, however, church and home life blended into one. This has both upsides and downsides. When church and home are essentially the same thing, there are no margins for façade. My siblings and I grew up seeing ministry from the inside out, in all its glory and grittiness. What I didn't realize at the time was how truly narrow our context was—even within the Christian world—and how unprepared I was for how it would feel to move outside it. In my naiveté, I didn't know there was anything to prepare *for.*

From Warren to World

At the outset of this chapter, I said that to recognize the cross of Christ reflected in the culture, we must be able to see society for what it is, understand the Christian's place in it, and see ourselves as both products of society and contributors to it.

My spiritual formation, while in some ways wonderful and amazing, did not prepare me for that sort of thinking. From my teachers at school, I learned to fear "the world," and from my parents and church, I learned that the world was alternately something to be cautious of and something to be evangelized. Neither is the complete story.

Fear Not

Christians are called neither to adopt society's mindset nor to reject society itself. Instead, we are called to live in it faithfully as called by Christ.

In his first epistle, Peter paints a picture of what this might look like. After developing the beautiful metaphor of God adding us brick by brick to his spiritual house, supported by our chief cornerstone Jesus, Peter says this:

> But you are a chosen race, a royal priesthood, a holy nation, a people for his own possession, *that you may proclaim the excellencies of him who called you out of darkness into his marvelous light.* Once you were not a people, but now you are God's people; once you had not received mercy, but now you have received mercy.
>
> Beloved, I urge you *as sojourners and exiles* to abstain from the passions of the flesh, which wage war against your soul. *Keep your conduct among the Gentiles honorable,* so that when they speak against you as evildoers, *they may see your good deeds and glorify God* on the day of visitation.

> Be subject for the Lord's sake to every human institution, whether it be to the emperor as supreme, or to governors as sent by him to punish those who do evil and to praise those who do good. For this is the will of God, *that by doing good you should put to silence the ignorance of foolish people. Live as people who are free, not using your freedom as a cover-up for evil, but living as servants of God.* Honor everyone. Love the brotherhood. Fear God. Honor the emperor.[9]

Among many truths expressed in this passage, we observe that even though we are set apart as members of God's spiritual family, we are still called to live righteous lives and verbally proclaim his excellencies *among those who are not like-minded.*[10]

The word *among* is so powerful. We're not called to form a separate society, blocked away from all who don't believe. Instead, we're called to live a separate kind of life while living *within society.* We don't silence the ignorance of foolish people by walling ourselves away from them. We do the opposite. We live among them, displaying good deeds and living freely as servants of God.

---

[9] 1 Peter 2:9-17. Emphasis mine.

[10] Since Peter's original audience was made up of early Christian converts from a Jewish background, he's using terms familiar to them to describe the people of God. All believers are now God's "chosen people" and have access to the accompanying rights and blessings. The term *Gentile* in this case means those who are not connected to Christ.

Another Kingdom

I'm telling you part of my story for a reason. Call it an origin story, if you will. A pedestrian one, for sure; but I want you to know where I'm coming from. For a long time, I felt as if I didn't truly belong anywhere. It made me feel weak, but in reality, it's part of what makes me strong. Though the details of our upbringings may not coincide, if you're also a follower of Christ, on this point we can all relate. We don't belong. And we're going to feel it.

Christ's Kingdom is not of this world, and though our culture of origin may determine our baseline thoughts and behavior, once our life in Christ begins, our conduct should no longer be shaped primarily by it. Instead, we conform ourselves to Christ's culture; and in him, we have nothing to fear—especially not earthly society.

The only thing Scripture commands us to fear is God himself, and the Christian who has been reconciled to God in Christ has nothing to fear from him.

> Having been justified by God, we need not fear divine condemnation (Romans 8:1). Having been chosen by God, we need not fear His rejection (Ephesians 1:4–6; Luke 12:32; Jude 1:24). With Christ as our Shepherd, we need not fear the valley of the shadow of death (Psalm 23:4). With the Maker of heaven

and earth watching over us, we need not fear anything (Psalm 121).[11]

Because Christ has reconciled us to the Father and the Holy Spirit is working in and through our lives, we can move in this world without fear. This, for the spiritually mature, should be what it means to live as both a Christian and a member of society.

While there's a healthy awareness of temptation, there's also the knowledge that he who lives within us is greater than he who is within the world. Though temptation will be ever-present, there is One who is also ever-present with us, who will provide a way of escape. We do not walk alone through the darkness. The Holy Spirit lives in us; the community of saints surrounds us; we bear the cross of Christ before us. To those who are perishing, the cross is foolishness; but to those who are being saved, it is the power of God.[12]

In Christ, we neither fear the culture nor allow its mindset to rule us. Understanding our secured place in an invisible, everlasting kingdom determines how we relate to society and move through it—and to live as faithful witnesses, we absolutely must do both.

A large part of how Christians navigate this world involves how we engage with its stories—fiction, nonfiction, our own real-life drama, and everything in between. In humanity's collective stories, we find reflections of the image of God and the eternal truths of Scripture, even

---

[11] "What Does the Bible Mean When It Tells Us to Fear Not?" *Got Questions*, https://www.gotquestions.org/fear-not.html (accessed April 21, 2020).
[12] 1 Corinthians 1:18.

in the stories of those who are perishing and will never acknowledge the Creator in their lifetimes. In one way or another, all stories connect back to the greatest Person who ever lived and the greatest story ever told.

Discussion Questions:

1. Did you grow up primarily in the culture, in the American Evangelical bubble, in Fundamentalism, or in something else? Briefly describe how this mindset has led you to view society and your place in it as a Christian.

    _____

    _____

    _____

2. Describe a time when you didn't "fit in." What happened? How has it affected you?

    _____

    _____

    _____

3. Which is more of a danger for you: fearing the culture or being ruled by its mindset? How do we overcome these extremes?

    _____

    _____

    _____

4. In what ways do the specifics of your upbringing still influence your spiritual formation and how you interact with society? What are the blessings associated with this? What are the challenges?

    _____

    _____

    _____

Notes

_____
_____
_____
_____
_____
_____
_____
_____
_____
_____
_____
_____
_____
_____
_____
_____
_____
_____
_____
_____
_____
_____
_____

Chapter 2

As a writer of fiction, I sometimes feel sorry for my characters. I do the worst things to them. I break their bones and ruin their plans and leave them cowering in blizzards, hiding from murderers. I spill their coffees and stab them with knives and drop spiders on their heads at the worst possible times. (Though it's hard to imagine a good time for that.) I don't just mess them up, however; I also help them learn and grow. I teach them vital lessons about relationships and faith. I set them in caring families, surround them with supportive friends, and help them find love.

My characters never suspect who's at the root of all this, however. They don't even know I exist. Though my presence permeates every page, I'm invisible to their eyes. They cannot and will not encounter me. Ever. They are my creation; and as their creator, I choose not to write myself into the narrative. The Author of our faith isn't like that, though. He wrote himself directly into our story.

Behold Our God

The very fact that we know anything at all about our Creator and what he is like is a sheer miracle. This is not hyperbole.

Our God is transcendent. He exists above and beyond human experience. If he hadn't chosen to reveal himself, there's no way we could have discovered him on our own. If he hadn't come to us, there's no way we could have reached him. If he hadn't redeemed us, there's no way we could have achieved righteousness on our own. Yet, for whatever reason, that's what God has done.

Though transcendent, God is also immanent. He made himself known to us, came to redeem us, and recorded the history of this redemptive narrative in a book. Through it all, the rightly named Author and Finisher of our faith has developed his redemption narrative as only the Origin of All Stories could.[13]

Setting

As novelist Eudora Welty has asserted, a story's setting is more than simply a picturesque backdrop. The setting is the very foundation on which all other story elements are built. In fact, without a strong sense of place rooting the narrative, there could be no story at all. Only after creating a backdrop with understandable rules, codes, and customs can the storyteller sensibly create the characters and shape the story.[14]

At the outset of this book, I took some time to tell you a little bit about myself and where I come from. You now have a sense of why I think the way I do and what factors have shaped my development. I do this not purely for practical purposes but for personal ones. You could even say theological ones. I establish the background because I want you to understand my story; and I want you to understand my story so that you will understand me. This is what God has done for us. He

---

[13] Hebrews 12:2.
[14] Eudora Welty, *On Writing* (New York: Modern Library, 2002), 41-45.

established a setting and told us a story—not as an end in itself but so that we could know and understand him.

Any time storytellers go through the process of establishing a sense of place and building their story outward from it, they mimic the actions of the God who made them. This is just as true for those who do not acknowledge their Creator as for those who do. Whether we recognize God's image stamped on us or not, we can't help looking like him. For those who love him, this truth resonates in profound ways. Particularly those of us who practice storytelling. We recognize our God as the ultimate creative and a master storyteller. He's been telling one story from Eden until now.

Creation is the backdrop against which he displays it. So many aspects of this backdrop give us hints of its maker. Our cosmos points to an ordered, caring, playful, and wise Designer. The unreachable outer edges of the universe indicate a mysterious transcendence, while the tangible blessings of life on earth suggest immanent attention. The intricate design of cells points to mathematical precision. The abundance of plant and animal life reveal a generous nature.[15] I could go on, but you get the drift.

The cosmological backdrop does more than give us clues about the Designer. It also speaks to the value he places on the story he's telling and the characters he works with. You don't create a setting so

---

[15] Or, as my friend Lucy reminded me one morning as we were watching the sun rise on the beach and marveling at the vast number of birds in the sky and fish in the sea, God is *extra*.

rich and vast unless you plan to propel a message that matters through characters worthy of love and cherishing. This is especially true of redemption's Protagonist.

After establishing a broad cosmological backdrop, God chose a specific, local setting in which to reveal his Son, Jesus Christ. The Christ could have appeared anywhere or at any time, yet the actual time and place of his arrival doesn't really seem logical from a human perspective. But settings are the basic building-blocks of a story. They tell you not only about the characters but about the nature of the story being told. Therefore, Jesus' setting holds critical truths we cannot lightly skim over.

It means something that God's son was born when and where he was—in the ancient Near East, say, instead of in modern-day Europe or the Americas. It means something that, although of noble lineage, the Christ did not live among the established elite. That he spent the helpless days of his early life on the continent of Africa, fleeing specific threats of violence. That his eventual hometown was the sort of place that instantly ignited people's prejudices ("Can anything good come out of Nazareth?").[16]

Story

As Holy Scripture, the Bible is unlike any other book. It is living and active. Through the power of the Holy Spirit, the Bible reveals the Godhead to us, convicting us of sin, righteousness, and judgment to

---

[16] John 1:46.

come.[17] From the Scriptures, we learn objective truth about who God is (facts he announces about himself) but also gain a somewhat subjective understanding of what he's like (observing how he interacts with his creation down through the ages).[18]

Yes, we learn Scripture; but we don't *just* learn information and facts. If so, we'd be in big trouble. Knowledge, we're told, puffs up.[19] When Scripture is worked into our hearts by the Spirit, however, we do much more than learn facts. We can also learn the fear of the Lord. This is the beginning of wisdom.[20]

When I was a child, I studied Scripture passages as little, self-contained stories. It did not occur to me that these smaller stories linked into a grander narrative of redemption that my story connected to as well. Only as I matured (both in age and the faith) did I recognize that each small story formed a grand, cohesive narrative encompassing God's total work across space and time. Thus began the feedback loop. As I grasped the grand design, the individual stories carried richer, deeper connections.

Understanding the grand narrative of Scripture this way helps us root our own stories within the greater scheme of things. Only after our

---

[17] Hebrews 4:12; John 16:8.

[18] I say *somewhat* subjective because although truth is not subjective, our full and total understanding of God (and, in relation to him, objective truth) will always be hampered and clouded in this life. This isn't the place to offer full examples, but the witness of church history speaks eloquently to this.

[19] 1 Corinthians 8:1.

[20] Proverbs 9:10.

stories are connected to the grand narrative can we grow in both knowledge (what happens) and wisdom (what it means).

- In reading God's sacrifice of a lamb for Adam and Eve in Genesis, we don't just learn *what happens* as a result. We come to recognize that God took the initiative toward redemption and restoration. We witness his grace and mercy.

- In reading the book of Ruth, we don't just learn *what happened* to two women. We also recognize that Yahweh cares in special ways for those on the margins of society. In this case, it's two widows, alone in the world and living as foreigners. First Naomi lives as a foreigner in Moab; then Ruth as a foreigner in Israel. In both cases, we recognize different aspects of God's mercy and grace. In Ruth's experience, we witness God working on behalf of one whose heart looks to him in eager anticipation; in Naomi's, we recognize him working in a heart overwhelmed by grief and plunged in despair. He sees, cares, and bestows favor on both.

- In watching Jonah grapple with his call to prophesy repentance to Nineveh, we don't just learn *what happened* when he disobeyed. We also note that the human heart desires mercy for self and judgment for others. While we may love the idea of a compassionate God in theory, we find it hard when God lavishes mercy on our own personal enemies. We observe, with fear and trembling, that the self-righteous would rather die than see God's mercy poured out on certain types of sinners.

- In witnessing Jesus' dialogue with the woman at the well, we don't just learn *what happened* when he spoke to her. We recognize that God takes women's theological questions seriously. Furthermore, he will go out of his way to engage directly with the social outcasts and isn't afraid of the blowback from his own community.

Our theology is not composed merely of truths we learn (orthodoxy) but involves how we apply them (orthopraxy). True faith is embodied faith. Even God himself became a Person.

Protagonist

In Jesus, we see the union of orthodoxy and orthopraxy. In his parables, he told truths; in his life, he lived them. In the Synagogues, he read from the Scriptures. In the streets, he fulfilled their prophecies.

People talk much today of living their truth, and it occurs to me that Jesus is perhaps the only person who's ever fully done that. As the Word made flesh, he embodied truth in a way none of us ever will. He was literal Truth, living, breathing, and walking among us.

This is our Protagonist. We behold his glory.[21]

Primary Audience

---

[21] John 1:14.

As an author of fiction, my job is not just to tell a story but to do so through characters who will seem real and relatable to my target audience. That last qualifier is key. No one character will be relatable to everyone. Genre expectations play a role in this. As an author of women's fiction, I find that the qualities making my characters relatable would feel out of place in a thriller or a detective novel. As storytellers, we must think about the type of people we're primarily telling our stories to, knowing that different qualities will be required to make my characters seem relatable *to those particular people.*

With that qualifier in mind, let's turn to the Author of the greatest story ever told. Who did he have in mind as his target audience when he divinely orchestrated the specifics of Jesus' life? In other words, what target audience is most likely to find Jesus relatable?[22]

The writer of Hebrews tells us that Jesus, as our High Priest, is able to sympathize with our human weaknesses. Let's consider how his earthly backdrop uniquely equips him to identify with weakness and suffering.

- Born into a precarious living situation
- Fled political violence
- Became a refugee

---

[22] Some might make the case that since God is Trinity, his primary audience is always the other members of the Godhead, with created beings, whether human and supernatural, being secondary or tertiary. That would be rather overthinking the nature of what we're doing here. In this section, we're considering the primary human audience of Scripture.

- Lived as a Jewish man, part of an ethnic minority oppressed under the Roman Empire
- Was not personally attractive
- Came of age as a backwater nobody in a small town that was the butt of jokes
- Was largely misunderstood, both by opponents and followers alike
- Despised and rejected
- A man of sorrows, acquainted with grief
- Wrongfully arrested
- Abandoned by friends and followers
- Falsely accused
- Unjustly sentenced
- Endured immense physical pain
- Summarily executed

Those who will find Jesus most relatable are those who suffer deeply, especially those who suffer in similar ways. Those who lead small, precarious lives. Those who are misunderstood, treated unjustly, rejected, and who suffer pain. In these ways in particular, the Savior relates to us—and we to him.

Jesus has lived in the middle of nowhere and been considered a nobody—even while knowing full well he was a Somebody. He was the original "prophet without honor in his own country." Jesus knows how it feels to be discounted by family, friends, and community.[23] He single-mindedly pursued a holy calling few others recognized and no other earthly companion fully understood. Jesus knows how it feels to suffer physically, mentally, emotionally, and spiritually. Though in a few key ways, Jesus is supremely unrelatable (the fact that he's sinless and God-in-the flesh are two biggies), in many other respects, so many of us will find his humble circumstances supremely relatable.

When you're tempted to question God's choice of setting for your life—the details that make existence painful or difficult—consider his choice of setting for his Son. Aspects of Jesus' setting both informed his story and shaped its outcome. The same is true for you. Consider all the ways in which suffering helps you relate to Jesus—and he to you.

This is why Jesus can say it is a blessing to be poor in spirit, mournful, meek, persecuted for righteousness' sake, and reviled without cause. The ones who suffer in these ways are the ones best positioned to see God and experience his reward.[24] These aspects of Christian life are a large part of what make the cross seem foolish to those who are perishing. But we can't adopt the world's mindset on this. We know the truth. For us who are being saved, the cross is the power of God. This is the greatest story ever told.

Discussion Questions:

---

[23] John 4:44.
[24] See Matthew 5.

1. Why is it appropriate to refer to the story of Jesus as "the greatest story ever told"?

   _____

   _____

   _____

2. In planning the formative years against which the Son would live out the story of redemption, the Father could have chosen any time or place. What are we to make of where, when, and how Jesus was born?

   _____

   _____

   _____

3. Why is it important to view individual narratives (whether within Scripture or our daily lives) in connection with the grand narrative of God revealing himself through redemptive history?

   _____

   _____

   _____

4. What do the specifics of Jesus' life reveal about who will and will not find Jesus a "relatable character"? What deeper

theological truths might this uncover about the greater story of redemption?

_____

_____

_____

Notes

_____

_____

_____

_____

_____

_____

_____

_____

_____

_____

_____

_____

_____

_____

_____

_____

_____

_____

_____

_____

_____

Chapter 3

|

As we discussed in the first chapter, I came of age pre-internet and socially out of the loop. Raised first in a farming community and then an underdeveloped Florida suburb, I had very little perspective on broader American culture. I read a lot of books, yes. But with limited exposure to television, popular radio, and movies, I sometimes felt that my siblings and I were the most sheltered children on earth.

These realizations only hit me when I was in proximity to non-sheltered kids. But there were kids more sheltered than we were. In our Fundamentalist school, my parents' *laissez faire* attitude toward the library was shocking to the faculty and staff. They may have a point. I mean, I did read *Flowers in the Attic.* But there are mothers and fathers who consider *any* sort of fiction questionable—even fiction that doesn't involve melodramatic kidnappings, torture, and cringey incest.[25]

Even once I exited Fundamentalist circles, I still met parents who did more than merely filter their children's reading choices: they outright rejected fiction as a viable option for Christians, believing

---

[25] Regarding *Flowers in the Attic*, I got what I deserved. The internalized heebie-jeebies of that particular reading experience have never left me. They match the horror I felt when I sneaked out of my room one night at my grandfather's house. I stood in the darkened hallway to watch whatever he was watching on TV—which happened to be *Tales from the Crypt.* I didn't sleep well for weeks and was inoculated against seeking more of the same. In both cases, the punishment fit the crime.

fiction to be a form of lying. They limited their kids' reading choices to biographies, history books, and other non-fiction work only.

Practicing Discernment

Though I've never had the responsibility of raising a child of my own, I have spent decades working with kids as a teacher and a nanny. I recognize that when it comes to shepherding children, there are lines to be drawn, hearts and minds to protect. I also recognize that not everyone agrees on where those lines should be placed, and how firmly.

This isn't just true for children. We all must exercise discernment in what we choose to engage with. But discernment goes beyond simply deciding what we take in. Discernment encompasses how we interact with it.

In her book *All That's Good*, Hannah Anderson reminds us that, at the most basic level, Christian discernment is developing a taste for what's good so that we may embrace and enjoy it.[26] Within that pursuit, choosing what to engage or not to engage with is not solely about deciding what's "worldly" and then avoiding it. It's allowing the Spirit to work within our hearts so that no matter what we're taking in, our inward and outward responses both align to the heart of Christ. In some cases, discernment does mean total avoidance—say, with porn. In other cases, discernment means participating in broad cultural intake with an

---

[26] Hannah Anderson, *All That's Good: Recovering the Lost Art of Discernment* (Chicago: Moody Press, 2018), 13, 30.

eye toward recognizing what's good and reflective of God's truth while also pushing back against what's wrong, bad, or misleading.

Contrary to what I commonly heard taught within Fundamentalism, "being worldly" isn't simply about what movies we watch or don't watch, which authors we read or don't read, the sort of music we listen to or don't listen to, what clothes we wear (or don't wear—haha), the hairstyles we flaunt or don't flaunt. As with all Jesus' teachings, his lessons on discernment bypass rules and go straight for the heart. That's why, as Anderson clarifies, combatting worldliness is not about simple avoidance but about walking in the Spirit.

At its essence, worldliness is a disposition of the heart—the belief that goodness comes from the immediate satisfaction of temporal desire. But because worldliness is a disposition of the heart, we can't simply retreat into religious contexts to escape it. We also can't rely on adopting certain positions or practices to avoid it—especially if we use them to avoid the more difficult task of examining our own hearts and motives. As long as we've picked the "right" education for our children, go to the "right" church, watch the "right" movies, and vote for the "right" candidate, we won't have to face the deeper truth about how easily our hearts are led astray. We could be consumerist, pragmatic, and completely worldly but never know it because we see our choices as "right" and thus are convinced that we are as well.[27]

In other words, a worldly mindset comes more from within than without. It is both a cause and an effect. While a worldly mindset can certainly be fed by the social artifacts we consume, it also can (and must!) be starved by the way the Spirit filters everything we take in. When we walk in the Spirit, we navigate this world always seeking what's good, right, and true while rejecting what's bad, wrong, and false.

As an avid reader of fiction over the years, I've read plenty of "clean" Christian stories that, though free of profanity or explicit sex scenes, absolutely do not tell the truth about various aspects of human nature—particularly relationships. Likewise, I've read books published in the general market that more accurately reflect the way people really are. Yet there are readers who will unquestionably swallow the former and reject the latter, all in the name of "discernment."

Tell Me Another

Okay, sure. If you want to get technical, fiction can be considered a lie. After all, it's not "the truth" in that it is made up. But it's also been said that fiction is the lie that tells the truth.[28] I assert that even God would agree. He gives us proof in Scripture.

---

[27] Ibid, 54.

[28] Garson O'Toole, "Art Is a Lie That Makes Us Realize Truth," *Quote Investigator,* https://quoteinvestigator.com/2019/10/29/lie-truth/ (accessed March 10, 2020).

When he initiated biblical authors, he did not prompt them only to record events in a strict, narrative fashion. He didn't even limit Scripture to narrative. The Bible reflects a full spectrum of genres, including poetry, allegory, songs, prophecies, personal and corporate letters, maxims, parables, fables, and even riddles.

Think of the way Jesus used parables in his public ministry. He would often tell a parable and let it stand for itself. Only later, when asked directly by his inner circle, would he discuss the meaning behind the parable. If the Word-Made-Flesh himself, the Way-Truth-and-Life, the Author and Finisher of our faith, can use fiction to tell the truth, then we who are made in his image can do likewise.

Fiction is not only a viable option for Christians but a necessary element in developing healthy imagination and empathy. As we will discover in the next chapter, all genres can reveal truths about human nature, help clarify our relationship to the God who made us, and allow us to express his glory.

The Tension

Though we often speak of fiction and nonfiction as opposites, they are actually complementary storytelling techniques that make the most sense in relationship to one another. This hearkens back to what Eudora Welty said about setting. Only once a recognizable backdrop has been established can we build a story outward from it.

Non-fiction stories help us learn more about our real-time setting. That knowledge better enables us to analyze fiction. The better we know this real world down to its bones, the better we're able to recognize whether it is or is not being accurately reflected in a story. Remember, fiction is a lie that tells the truth. When fiction fails to do that, we're disappointed, and rightly so. But it is only through a breadth and depth of experiencing reality that we are better able to make those observations.

The stories we love, the ones that become timeless classics, are the ones that connect in some way to our real, actual lives. The best fiction stories carry the unmistakable ring of truth. Take fantasy literature as one example. Though it may contain profoundly unrealistic story elements, it often explores deep epistemological questions. The characters' names are often hard to pronounce and the settings exotic, but the issues explored in such stories are ones we would recognize no matter the context. We've lived versions of them ourselves. We may differ from the characters in obvious ways—they might not even be human—but at their core, they resemble well-known archetypes from our own world.

Though most will not go to the extreme of saying Christians should not read fiction, many behave functionally as if this were true. Feeling that non-fiction is somehow more intelligent or more noble, they ignore a wealth of rich and nourishing storytelling. While lifestyle and temperament may predispose us to preferring one over the other, we must not abandon either. Fiction and nonfiction work not in competition with one another but in concert.

Deep down, though, we're all looking for the same sorts of things in our stories. We want reality accurately reflected—to be rooted more firmly in this life, shown instances of confidence and courage, be given hope that we, too, can struggle and survive. But we also want our imagination captured—to be drawn out of our own experiences, shown miracles and wonders, be given hope for a new and better world.

For the Christian, fiction allows us to indulge even deeper longings. "Fiction allows something non-fiction cannot—the envisioning of ideal people, places, worlds that simply do not exist in reality because of the effects of sin. Fiction enables us to picture a world without sin or a world in which God's character and values can be imagined untainted by sin. To be able to envision ideals like this is a valuable aspect of fiction."[29]

This is what stories can do. When we exercise discernment—when we look for what's good—the stories we love, no matter the medium or genre, can provide opportunities to connect more deeply with ourselves, our society, and our God. All we need are eyes to see the connections.

Discussion Questions:

1. In this chapter, discernment is defined as "developing a taste for what's good so that we may embrace and enjoy it." How does

---

[29] Young-Sam Won, e-mail message to author, June 11, 2020.

this definition compare with how you've traditionally thought about discernment?

_____

_____

_____

2. How does fiction help us understand real life, and how does real life help us better enjoy and analyze fiction?

_____

_____

_____

3. Can fiction and non-fiction both effectively help communicate spiritual realities? If yes, in what ways? If no, why not?

_____

_____

_____

4. Why are both fiction and non-fiction necessary for healthy learning and human expression?

_____

_____

_____

Notes

_____

_____

_____

_____

_____

_____

_____

_____

_____

_____

_____

_____

_____

_____

_____

_____

_____

_____

_____

_____

_____

_____

_____

PART II

Chapter 4

My time adjacent to Fundamentalism ingrained into me the idea that discernment was primarily about avoidance. We could only remain "godly" by staying separated from the culture. At the Fundamentalist school that I attended, this was both taught explicitly and demonstrated implicitly.

My junior year of high school, our school actually had our literature books unbound and rebound. The school even had their own on-site print shop in which they accomplished this task. Why go to all this trouble? So that they could remove a lengthy excerpt from *The Scarlet Letter.*

As high school students, most of us were thrilled that our textbooks were now thinner and our classwork lighter as a result. As an adult Christian who's not only read *The Scarlet Letter* but taught it in high school classrooms, I'm still shaking my head over this nonsensical decision.

For those needing a refresher, *The Scarlet Letter* is an American novel by Nathaniel Hawthorne. First published in 1850, it's the story of a woman "caught" in adultery in a Puritan town, shunned by the community, yet unwilling to name the man who fathered her child. Unlike the steamy movie trailers of film adaptations would have you believe, the book contains no sex scenes. By the time our story picks up, the adultery has long since passed, and the characters are now dealing with the fallout. And make no mistake—there is fallout.

The storyline draws out major themes of guilt, shame, repression, and redemption, and the way in which Hawthorne sets these elements against a Puritan backdrop provides interesting points of connection and contrast with the true Gospel of Christ. These were discussions my classmates and I were destined never to have, however. Within Fundamentalist thinking, *The Scarlet Letter* was deemed "bad"—and therefore something to be avoided.

But cultural artifacts aren't something to be avoided. Evaluated? Often. Confronted? Sometimes. But the idea that we can avoid the culture is not just impractical—it's a myth. If you buy into this sort of thinking, you're cutting yourself off from more than the things that you think will harm you. You're depriving yourself of the very skills you need to develop actual discernment.

Discernment involves the ability to judge things and people well.[30] While discernment may include dismissing certain cultural artifacts out of hand, it also means so much more than that. Discernment also means learning to pick things apart, piece by piece, weighing them in the balance. It means investigating what is true, what's not true, and how truths are reflected in the stories we create and consume.

---

[30] *Cambridge Dictionary*, s.v. "Discernment," https://dictionary.cambridge.org/us/dictionary/english/discernment (accessed May 21, 2020).

Instead of using "discernment" to decide ahead of time if stories are "good" or "bad," I now think more in terms of what stories can reveal. What can we learn about the hopes, fears, and dreams of humankind? About God, society, and ourselves? Are these feelings universal across ages, continents, and cultures? How do our stories connect to the greatest story ever told?[31]

By "the greatest story ever told," I refer to Father God sending his son Jesus, to a specific time and place to fulfill a specific purpose. That purpose was the redemption of human souls and eventual restoration of all creation. Though we have already experienced a partial fulfillment of this restoration, one day we will enjoy the complete benefits. We will experience spiritual unity with the Godhead, unified connections with humankind, and a transformed relationship with creation and all living creatures. In one way or another, the stories we tell betray deep longings for these future realities. Some do so consciously, some subconsciously.

Beginning in this section, we will explore different literary genres, mining them for universal truths and connecting them to the truth of the gospel.

---

[31] Again, I'd like to offer the caveat that yes, there certainly are stories or modes of storytelling I will dismiss out of hand because I find them unbecoming of a believer. I've already given porn as an example in an earlier chapter, but here I might add movies or books that obviously and unashamedly glorify perversions. Though all things are lawful, not all things are beneficial. 1 Corinthians 6:12 and Philippians 4:8 must synthesize in our hearts under the guidance of the Holy Spirit.

Brace yourselves. You're about to have an avalanche of allusions flying straight at your face. Literary and cinematic, classic and prosaic, big and small screen—all in a giant jumble, barreling straight at you. Some you will recognize; some you won't. Enjoy the former and don't worry too much about the latter.

Here we go.

Action and Adventure

Action and adventure stories always have clearly defined villains, victims, and heroes.[32] The hero is quickly pitted against a masterful and overwhelmingly powerful force. Sometimes this force is a person, sometimes an element of nature, sometimes a powerful conspiracy. Whatever the enemy, it is the hero's job to defeat it and rescue helpless victims.

The villain seems undefeatable. Everyone knows it will take nothing short of a miracle to save the day. Enter the hero. He'll have something special about him that sets him apart and puts him in a position to shift the balance of power. These heroes bear the brunt of fighting evil, but usually don't fight alone. More often, the hero merely evens the playing field somehow, liberating other would-be victims and empowering them to join the fight.

As I worked on this section, the first thing that came to mind was Marvel's *Avengers: Endgame.* (Likely because I'm writing during

---

[32] And heroines, of course. Sticking with one form of the word to simplify writing, but I see you, ladies.

COVID-19 quarantine and have been re-watching the franchise. I should warn you that the rest of this paragraph contains mild spoilers.) In the final battle scenes, our heroes face certain defeat. They are clearly outmatched by Thanos. Despite having the power of godlike beings, the Avengers are losing.[33] The tide turns only by the arrival of Stephen Strange. He does something for the rest of the Avengers that they could never do for themselves, and only then does their position shift from would-be victims to an empowered army.[34]

In telling and consuming action and adventure stories, we reflect two inborn human desires: the need to be rescued and the desire to become rescuers. We both long for a real-life T'Challa or Shuri, and we desire to become them ourselves. (#WakandaForever)

In the gospel, we see a Rescuer standing against the powerful, evil forces of sin, death, and hell, fighting for those who cannot save themselves. He frees them from their yoke of bondage, empowering them to join him in his good fight as he makes all things new.

Fantasy

Fantasy stories are known for richly built, otherworldly settings. Against these lush backdrops, a daunting task will be paired with a straightforward solution. For example: The One Ring is evil, and we must drop it in lava. How simple! Of course, all is not as it seems. This

---

[33] Yes, some are actually gods. Quit interrupting, nerds.
[34] If that last battle scene doesn't give you apocalyptic End-Times feels, I don't know what will. I mean, other than C.S. Lewis's novel *The Last Battle*.

53

seemingly simple solution is fraught with many obstacles and opportunities for failure. As in *The Lord of the Rings*, the initial simplicity of the plot quickly unfolds in nesting-doll-style subplots. Over hundreds of pages, complications unfold in rich and perilous layers.

Along the way, humans and godlike beings mingle with sentient animals and mythical creatures. Fantasy stories typically contain magical and supernatural elements, and the best ones set clear rules and limits. Despite the possibility of supernatural powers, no characters are completely immune to pain, failure, suffering, or death. Except perhaps the villains. In fantasy literature, villains are the strongest and most powerful beings, seemingly invincible.

Power structures always play a strong role in these sorts of stories. Plots are riddled with authoritative governments, influential guilds, majestic kingdoms, and compelling individual leaders, be they human or supernatural. The ways in which power structures operate both define our characters and set up forces either against them or in their favor. Often, such stories play with distance and proximity, forcing two characters with great social distance into intimate connections. Enemies-to-friends is a common relational development, and unlikely pairings often infuse humor and heart into otherwise bleak moments. Consider the friendship of Gimli the dwarf and Legolas the elf.

When we create and consume these types of stories, we betray some of our deepest longings. We yearn to be part of something greater than ourselves—something otherworldly and beyond this life. We long for good to triumph over evil. We crave deep and strong connections, both with our fellow humans and with nature—specifically, with animals. What child hasn't dreamed of being best friends with a talking horse, solving crimes with a know-it-all cat, whispering secrets to our puppy best friend—and having the puppy whisper back?

Tim Keller has written a solid essay on this topic. In it, he points out that although fantasy stories are often far-fetched on the surface, they speak to very real hungers.

> The great fairy tales and legends—"Beauty and the Beast," "Sleeping Beauty," King Arthur, Faust—did not really happen, of course. They are not factually true. And yet they seem to fulfill a set of longings in the human heart that realistic fiction can never touch or satisfy. That is because deep in the human heart there are these desires—to experience the supernatural, to escape death, to know love that we can never lose, to not age but live long enough to realize our creative dreams, to fly, to communicate with nonhuman beings, to triumph over evil. If the fantasy stories are well told, we find them incredibly moving and satisfying. Why? It is because, even though we know that factually the stories didn't happen, our hearts long for these things…Our hearts sense that even though the stories themselves

aren't true, the underlying realities behind the stories are somehow true or *ought to be*.[35]

When we create and consume these types of stories, we acknowledge a deep-rooted desire to experience something beyond physical reality. For a meeting of the natural and the supernatural. To see miracles and wonders. Purely secular and physical experiences, on their own, are not fully satisfying. Buried in every human heart is an awareness that there's an underlying spiritual reality. They sense that the way the world is right now is not necessarily the way it ought to be.

As Keller points out in another section of his essay, this is where the story of Christ's arrival on this earth really speaks to us. At the core, Advent is the story of a god becoming human—in this case, the *actual God* becoming an *actual man*, Jesus. As the God-man, he will fulfill ancient prophecies, heal the sick, raise the dead, die, and come back from the dead.

This Story, the best of all stories, hits all the notes of these underlying longings and realities. But unlike a fairy tale, the Advent story doesn't begin with "once upon a time." Instead, the account recorded factually in Matthew's Gospel "says that this is no fairy tale. Jesus Christ is not one more lovely story pointing to these underlying realities—Jesus *is* the underlying reality to which all the stories point."[36]

---

[35] Timothy Keller, *Hidden Christmas: The Surprising Truth Behind the Birth of Christ* (New York: Viking, 2016), 25-26.
[36] Ibid., 27.

Science Fiction

People tend to lump fantasy and science fiction together, but they are two distinct genres with different storytelling expectations. While both go beyond the experiences of daily life, Science Fiction roots at least one of its major plot elements on science. This may be hard science or social science, real or hypothetical, proven or theoretical. Some people actually prefer the term *Speculative Fiction*, since such stories speculate what would happen if scientific advances were possible, made, or carried out to the nth degree.

- "What if the government eliminates shared public memory and redefines words?" asks George Orwell in *1984.*

- "What if there were such a thing as a tesseract?" wonders Madeleine L'Engle in *A Wrinkle in Time*.

- "What might time travel reveal about society, my family, and myself?" explores Octavia E. Butler in *Kindred*.

As in fantasy, Science Fiction requires a certain degree of worldbuilding and rule-setting; however, unlike in fantasy, speculative stories are rooted not in imaginary realms but in our real, actual cosmos. Just one that's been dramatically altered somehow, either by human choice or by a new and powerful force.

To engage with Science Fiction is to tacitly acknowledge human fallibility. We are not all-seeing nor all-knowing. Even our best-laid plans will somehow go awry. Innovation alone cannot save us.

Humankind cannot fix the world without outside help, and hubristic attempts to do so will lead to unintended consequences. Technological innovations run amok, daydreams descend into nightmares, and utopian dreams devolve into dystopias.

These stories always leave me with mixed emotions. On the one hand, the complicated and bittersweet endings paint a bleak picture of human nature, leaving me feeling helpless and fraught. On the other hand, such stories can also provoke thankfulness to my Creator, who does not leave us to destroy ourselves. Time and again, he's intervened to save us from the worst extent of our own foolish choices.

While utopia is not possible in this life, I can look forward to the true, eternal reality spoken of by the prophets in Scripture. The Creator will make all things new by his own power, in his own way, and in due time.[37]

Horror

Horror stories purposefully invoke a sense of dread. They may include fantastical creatures and paranormal elements; but unlike fantasy, instead of arousing wonder and longing, these elements instill fear. These fears might include the supernatural (Bram Stoker's *Dracula*), the natural (Stephen King's *The Stand*) or the unknown (Josh Malerman's *Bird Box*).

As the plot unfolds, the characters themselves are kept in as much suspense as the audience, grappling with high stakes leading to

---

[37] See especially Isaiah 11, Matthew 25, and Revelation 21.

inevitable disaster. Two staples of this genre are the Gross Out and the Jump Scare. These emotionally high-voltage moments are intended either to revolt audiences with gore or startle them out of their seats. For classic examples, see Yeon Sang-ho's *Train to Busan* or Gore Verbinski's *The Ring*. This is what I'm told, anyway.

As someone who can barely tolerate this brand of storytelling, I struggle to understand what draws people back for more. And by "barely tolerate," I mean I was scared for a month after accidentally seeing the trailer for Jordan Peele's *Us*. The *trailer*.

Despite knowing that there's a neurological link between fear and reward and that people enjoy an emotional rush after safely confronting fears,[38] I take every opportunity to opt out of these experiences. I am baffled that others choose differently.

I asked a few Christians what draws them to horror, and here's what they said:

- "In horror, sometimes I think we need to find similarities between the dark of ourselves and the dark of the genre. But that opens a whole can of worms of what do to with that darkness. I think there's also a desire to be saved...whether by the book ending, by the hero rescuing the characters from the violence, or what have you. We

---

[38] Maya Dorn, "Scare Me, I Dare You: A Neuropsychological Account of the Horror Film," https://wesscholar.wesleyan.edu/cgi/viewcontent.cgi?article=3270&context=etd_hon _theses (accessed March 20, 2020).

like to see the saving, the reconciliation, the evil not win out. I know that's not true of all horror, but I think it's in there. Again, we have the ultimate Savior right in front of us, but I also think we often don't know (or don't want to know) just how horrific our sins are, so our Savior isn't as appealing. That is *not* to say horror is all bad and is replacing our Savior and we should give it up. I do think some horror is truly bad for the soul, but I don't think that can be totally generalized."[39]

- "I think the jolt of emotion they offer gives us an insight to our own motives and personalities, maybe even aspects of ourselves we don't like, but that doesn't mean that part of us doesn't exist. I think horror does a good job of leveling the playing field of human beings. When you get a really well-done horror story you are able to experience a human being in different emotional states, see their motives, and understand why they would make a decision they made. A great example of this is Wendy in *The Shining* (the book, not the film). The book gives her more of a backstory; she becomes a character that is easier to empathize with as opposed to her on screen portrayal. Even Jack is more human in the book than the movie. He's an alcoholic, he's a failure, but he is living

---

[39] Fayelle Ewuake, e-mail message to author, May 27, 2020.

with the same fears a lot of us are living with. What if we aren't as good as we thought we were? What if we don't have anything to offer? How are we going to live with our failures when they seem to keep repeating themselves?"[40]

- "Some thrillers are interesting and exciting and utterly implausible. That can make for the perfect opportunity to move out of my own worries and cares into a make-believe world where folks are up against insurmountable odds (example: *A Quiet Place*). There's something satisfying in some of these movies where the good guys "win." That doesn't always happen in real life — at least in ways we can tangibly see right now. Ultimately, of course, we know that the Lord works all things together for good for those that love Him and have been called according to His purposes, but that doesn't mean that everything that happens is good. Seeing someone make it through a crazy situation can be exciting and hopeful."[41]

- "I really like the old horror films that made me think differently. They were more about the human condition and less about evoking a polyvagal effect. I think they

---

[40] Marissa Jancovic, e-mail message to author, May 19, 2020.
[41] Anonymous, e-mail message to author, May 19, 2020.

make it clear that everyone can be a hero and a villain and I could use more of that kind of thinking in my life: I've always tried to make my faith and my life easy to compartmentalize, but that's just not how life is. Everything may not be as it seems."[42]

- "I love ghost stories, supernatural thrillers and some "romanticized vampire" novels/films (which are really just a version of the famed Byronic hero/tortured soul archetype). I have actually had several paranormal/supernatural experiences in my life, and one that was quite frightening, so I think there's a part of me that seeks to understand or explain those events. Edgar Allen Poe wrote horror because he sought to understand life after death. I think for me it's more of how life and death and evil intersect. *The Conjuring* is one of my favorite films. It is a fabulous depiction of the power of God through the name of Jesus. There is an exorcism enacted in the film, and they make no bones about the fact that Christ drives out demons and they cannot stand in His presence. These people were truly tormented because of the house's history, and it really showed that

---

[42] Becky L. McCoy, e-mail message to author, May 21, 2020.

demons are real and they set out to destroy lives. Every time I watch it, I feel like it galvanizes my faith."[43]

While working on this chapter, I also connected with Blake I. Collier, who has written for years on the subjects of horror and faith. Here's some of what he had to say.

> Most of my writing is exploring how horror connects with the traditional Christian faith. Because of how I view the genre, I find that most of the questions that I often ponder in the space of horror are ones surrounding doubt and hope. We've seen in reality how overly zealous brothers and sisters of the faith can lose grip with compassion, tradition, the Christian community as a whole, to the point that their belief in the unseen can splinter off into conspiracy theories and worldviews that ultimately counter the very claims of Christ, who is the center of the Christian faith. So, I often think about what would need to take place in order for those characters in these tales of horror that see the supernatural or creatures to relay their faith to those who are skeptical in a way that their fears would be, at least, rendered as palpable. The interplay of doubt about what we have experienced and the hope that someone will believe us and help us (hope) is something I think about a lot.
>
> However, that is just one area that I think about.

---

[43] Megan Whitson Lee, e-mail message to author, May 20, 2020.

There is some debate as to whether it would be considered horror or not, but there is a scene at the end of *Take Shelter* (2011) where the family man who is the main protagonist of the film has gone through a disruption in this life throughout the runtime of the film. The audience is never sure if he is losing his mind or if these events are actually taking place, but at the end of the film, the father's visions are witnessed by his daughter (who is hard of hearing) and his wife and that scene brings me to tears every time. It's the idea that his family can share in his fear, in his doubt, in his faith, that they can see what he sees and be with him, live with him, and walk with him in that space whether it is real or he is going through some form of mental illness. It's beautiful and has spoken to the beauty of sharing a common faith with my fellow brothers and sisters in Christ, but also in a very practical sense of walking with my own father as he slowly succumbs to early onset Alzheimer's.[44]

These perspectives were enlightening for me, especially since so many of them highlight the darkness of the human condition and the need for hope and salvation. In producing and consuming horror stories, we tacitly admit that deep down, we fear evils both natural and supernatural—the living and the dead (and the undead). We fear things

---

[44] Blake Collier, e-mail message to author, May 21, 2020.

that exist, things that do not exist, and things that likely never will. We fear what we can see and what we cannot—what we believe possible and what we hope is not.

In the end, it seems the spiritually inclined and the secularists aren't that different after all. We betray a shared fear of what lies just beyond our known reality. There's more to the cosmos than what we see; and in our hearts, we know it, even if we can't name it. Horror teases out these fears.

Christian theology gives us a sense of what we're in for. Scripture both confirms our worst fears and assuages them, affirming that we do not wrestle merely against flesh and blood, "but against the rulers, against the authorities, against the cosmic powers over this present darkness, against the spiritual forces of evil in the heavenly places."[45] That's the bad news. The good news of the gospel is that we are not left on our own to fight evil. Christ fights for us. If we're united with him, we can "be strong in the Lord and in the strength of his might," clothed in spiritual armor that will protect us against the devil's schemes.[46]

Mystery

In a mystery story, the major plotline follows a person or group trying to solve a crime while the culprit(s) work to keep it covered up. In these stories, there's more going on than simply creating characters

---

[45] Ephesians 6:10-12.
[46] Ibid.

to enact a plot. Writers are in an unspoken relationship with their readers and viewers. The audience understands that the all-knowing author sets up this sort of story as a puzzle for them to decode; but they're also aware that even if they solve the mystery before the in-story detectives do, they're powerless to intervene. Story creators generally intend for audiences to figure it out just before the dramatic final scenes, as danger reaches a boiling point and the bottled-up villain slowly (often dangerously) unravels.

A popular subset of this genre is the Cozy Mystery. As the title suggests, these offer more lighthearted fare, with the deaths happening largely off-stage. In a Cozy Mystery, the central characters run around collecting clues as if they're on a scavenger hunt, keeping the audience intrigued without forcing them to interact with the darker elements of the plot. Most Agatha Christie novels fall into this category. Think of her fictional sleuths Miss Marple and Hercule Poirot, who work mysteries out from the comfort of their armchairs while chatting with suspects and sipping endless cups of tea. Meanwhile, at the opposite of the spectrum, are Psychological Thrillers. These mysteries drop us directly into the center of the terrifying action, forcing us to grit our teeth and keep up (Jeong You-Jeong's *The Good Son)*.

No matter the subcategory, most mystery stories share one common element—a vivid backdrop. Think how many popular ones are set against the backdrop of quaint English hamlets or dark Scandinavian winters. It's not that country hamlets or icy forests host more crimes than other places in the world. It's that within this storytelling genre, a strong and distinct sense of place figures into the story. Those locations supply it. So does Miami Beach, the backdrop for USA's *Burn Notice*, Colombia Pictures' *Bad Boys* franchise, and a slew of paperback novels.[47] Within a quintessential mystery, the setting both sparks the imagination and feeds directly into the story. South Florida provides this in spades. Car chases along Miami Beach. Bodies dumped in the Everglades. Crime scenes only accessible by airboat. That sort of thing.

Whatever the backdrop, mysteries will typically feature some version of the lovable female sleuth, young or old (Nancy Drew, Mrs. Polifax), the relationally hampered male investigator (Inspector Wallander), or the quirky detecting team (the Scooby Gang). The strengths and weaknesses of the central mystery-solvers are offset by complementary sidekicks, acting either as intellectual foils (Holmes-Watson in the Sherlock Holmes stories), as emotional ballast (Booth-Brennan in *Bones*), or some combination of the two (Mulder-Scully in *The X-Files*).

The cases will seem convoluted at first, but there's always a simple solution. The clues are purposefully presented in the most obscure way possible to build suspense; but by the end of a good mystery, characters' choices are shown to be more or less logical,

---

[47] And yes, okay, *Miami Vice.* What year is this?

though evil.[48] The trick to building tension in a mystery story, then, is in how the storyteller dispenses crucial clues. Using narrative misdirection and sleight-of-hand, the narrator must decide exactly when and how to dole out information. She will release clues in maddeningly irregular intervals, mixing them with red herrings. Red herrings are "clues" inserted in the storyline intended to be distracting to the armchair sleuths following along. Storytellers must be judicious in their use. Here's the fun part. Since mystery audiences expect red herrings, master storytellers can actually play on these expectations and leverage them to further advantage. They do so by painting the red herrings as genuine and passing off genuine clues as red herrings. It all gets very twisty.

Dwight Schrute actually explains this well. Yes, Dwight Schrute of Dunder Mifflin. We'll hear more about him when we discuss comedy. For now, I want to highlight a particular comment he makes in Season 6 of *The Office*. While role-playing a part in the fictional board game "Belles, Bourbon, and Bullets," Dwight tells the documentary crew why he doesn't suspect the character "Voodoo Mama Juju," role-played by Angela, as the killer: "I know she didn't do it. *It's never the person you most suspect.* It's *also never the person you least suspect*, since anyone with half a brain would suspect them the most. Therefore, I know the

---

[48] We all have bones to pick with mysteries that, seemingly for the sake of twists, will manipulate the characters' choices in ways that stretch believability. Most recently for me was the 2019 Netflix Original *The Stranger*, based on a Harlan Coben novel by the same title.

killer to be Phyllis, a.k.a. Beatrix Bourbon, the person I most medium suspect."[49] Dwight succinctly states a dynamic we all recognize. When unraveling a whodunit, we know it can't be the person who *seems* like a killer since the genre demands that the mystery be more complex. Therefore, we view every character through a lens of suspicion, usually settling on someone the clues don't favor at the moment.

Part of our brain yearns to box things up and label them neatly. Maybe we're apt to fear the man in the black hoodie and automatically let down our guard for the woman in the white sundress. To believe children and doubt adults. To mistrust people who have certain accents, certain skin tones, and certain habits while responding comfortably to those who look and behave in ways we're already familiar with.

But these instincts cannot ultimately be trusted. As finite beings, we are truly limited in our ability to gather and parse information. Our first impressions and our gut instincts, though helpful perhaps as a starting point, can and should not be wholly trusted. The people we instinctively like upon first meeting might ultimately betray us, while those who make questionable first impressions could one day turn into our saviors. I'm not just talking about implicit biases, either, although I do think they affect us more than we suspect. I'm talking about people not turning out to be who we think they are.

---

[49] *The Office.* "Murder." Season 6, Episode 10. Directed by Greg Daniels. Written by Greg Daniels and Daniel Chun. NBC, 12 November, 2009. Emphasis mine.

These reversals don't just happen because our perceptions are off-base. They also happen because people are not static beings—they grow and change over the course of a lifetime. Even just over the past decade in my own life, I've been surprised by who's helped me and who's hurt me. I've been shaken all over again, reminded that we never can be completely certain of the hero-villain breakdown. We must wait for them to reveal themselves. And there are always surprises.

Just as mystery readers work in silent relationship to an all-knowing author, Christians live in relationship with the all-knowing Author of our faith. We worship a God we cannot see but whom we trust to write our stories. Consumers of mystery stories wait for the author's final plot revelations, and we wait for God to do something similar.

Paul wrote this in a letter to the ancient Roman church. Note the language of waiting, longing, and hope for God's revelation:

> For I consider that the sufferings of this present time are not worth comparing with the glory that *is to be revealed to us*. For the creation waits with *eager longing for the revealing* of the sons of God. For the creation was subjected to futility, not willingly, but because of him who subjected it, in hope that the creation itself will be set free from its bondage to corruption and obtain the freedom of the glory of the children of God. For we know that the whole creation has been groaning together in the pains of childbirth until now. And not only the creation, but we ourselves, who have the firstfruits of the Spirit, groan inwardly

as *we wait eagerly* for adoption as sons, the redemption of our bodies. For in this hope we were saved. Now hope that is seen is not hope. For who hopes for what he sees? But if we hope for what we do not see, *we wait for it with patience.*[50]

The Author and Finisher of our faith knows the end from the beginning. He knows what he's doing. We live in mystery not because we don't trust him but because of our own limited knowledge of when and exactly how he will accomplish his ultimate purposes. Sometimes all we know is that *one day we will know.* Better still, one day our eyes will behold him, and will be like him, for we will see him as he is.

Meanwhile, here we are. Still mid-story. We do not know the red herrings we will face along the way, what twists are still coming, and how we may be affected by surprise heroes, unexpected villains, and misdirection. We move forward in faith, waiting for the ultimate of all mysteries—the revealing of the kingdom of God.[51]

Discussion Questions:

1. Of the five genres discussed in this chapter, which ones tend to draw you in the most and keep you coming back for more? Why do you think that is?

---

[50] Romans 8:18-25, emphasis mine.
[51] Mark 4:11.

_____

_____

_____

2. What spiritual connections from this chapter caught your attention?

_____

_____

_____

3. What further spiritual parallels can you draw from stories in these genres?

    a. Action and Adventure

_____

_____

_____

    b. Fantasy

_____

_____

_____

    c. Science Fiction

_____

_____

_____

d. Horror

_____

_____

_____

e. Mystery

_____

_____

_____

Notes

_____

_____

_____

_____

_____

_____

_____

_____

_____

_____

_____

_____

_____

_____

_____

_____

_____

_____

_____

_____

_____

_____

Chapter 5

|

Our last chapter focused on fictional genres rooted in situations we're less likely to encounter. In this chapter, we'll explore stories set a bit closer to home. In dramas, historical fiction, realistic fiction, and comedies, we recognize slices of our daily lives. In these cultural artifacts, we'll also witness reflections of the cross.

Drama

In dramas, relatable characters live out real-life scenarios, learning and growing as they go. They face interpersonal struggles, work stresses, and complicated family situations, often while grappling with their own past trauma.

Though dramas may focus on one particular character, there are not the same neatly defined roles of heroes and villains that we see in Action and Adventure. Instead, most dramas feature an emotionally messy crew, with each character fighting personal battles. These characters generally have both internal and external struggles, meaning there will be dual storylines. A strong overarching plot, like the need to save the family home from foreclosure, will be paired with an inner journey, such as the need to heal from grief. These inner and outer journeys are connected, affecting one another symbiotically. As characters heal in one area, they're in a better position to resolve their other issues. Though the connection may seem obvious to onlookers, it often plays out without the character seeming to be aware.

These dynamics are especially evident in the American TV series *LOST*. While containing elements of Fantasy and Action and Adventure, this six-season juggernaut is a drama at its core. The overarching plot centers on a group of plane-crash survivors. Initially, viewers believe the story is about how they will escape a mysterious island. However, as the series progresses, it becomes clear that each character must overcome internal struggles linked to past hurts, revealed to viewers through extensive flashbacks. As we peel back the layers of internal struggles, we come to sympathize and root for them to grow and change *and* to escape the island.[52]

In creating and consuming dramas, we acknowledge that problems do not just come from the outside. They also come from within. While evil forces beyond our control can wreck our lives, inner conflicts contribute to the chaos. The dual conflicts in dramas point toward a reality most of us don't want to face. Even if all the outer problems we're facing were somehow wiped away, that would not be enough to cure our inner conflicts—*and vice versa*.

In this respect, dramas demonstrate a powerful truth of the gospel. Sin has both internal and external effects; therefore, practical solutions to our tangible, outer problems cannot prove sufficient for true human flourishing. What we need is a synthesis of internal and external healing. We find that healing in Christ.

---

[52] Though *LOST*'s format was addictive, I couldn't endure the show long-term. I tapped out after a few seasons and read a summary once the finale aired. I still have questions.

Historical Fiction

As the term implies, Historical Fiction sets characters against the backdrop of the real, actual past.[53] Though some of these stories incorporate actual historic figures, more often the main characters are ordinary people living through extraordinary times.

As with dramas, historical fiction pairs external upheavals with internal shifts. Characters fall in love during war or come of age during a pandemic. In Christian publishing, many historical fiction novels are also romances; but historical fiction need not necessarily factor love lines into its development.

Regardless of the emotional arcs, well-crafted historical fiction pays close attention to the manners, customs, and particular developments of a specific time. These works differ from what we now call "classics" in that the classics were generally set in the time contemporary to when they were published.[54] This is important to note because though classics are set in *our* past, the authors wrote contemporarily with their own time and therefore lack the benefit of

---

[53] Though it's not a genre we'll explore in much detail here, Alternate History stories explore the past's great "what if's." What if Hitler didn't die in that bunker? What if Alexander Hamilton had become President and worked to outlaw slavery? Fascinating in their own way, Alternate Histories require a strong working knowledge of real, actual events and therefore appeal to niche audiences.

[54] There are exceptions to this. Historical novels started popping up in English in the eighteenth and nineteenth centuries, meaning there are now-classics which were considered historical when they were written. But we're painting with very broad brushes just now, as you have no doubt noticed.

hindsight—an aspect of storytelling writers of historical fiction work to great advantage.

Engaging with stories set in the past allows us to operate outside the characters' timelines. In doing so, we can peer into their future and know how everything works out in the end—at least, how everything works out within the closed system of history. With the benefit of perspective, writers of historical fiction can do a few things for the people of the past that their own contemporary storytellers could not.

- They can lend dignity to historically marginalized social groups like Alice Walker does in *The Color Purple*.
- They can infuse a story with an inevitable sense of dread, deepened all the more because the characters themselves can't anticipate it. To see this done well (and to have your emotions destroyed in the process) see Elizabeth Wein in *Code Name Verity*.
- They can highlight irony between the characters' expectations and the cold reality of fact, as seen in the BBC series *The Crown*.
- They can reveal layers of history that our textbooks have largely omitted, as Linda Sue Park does in *Prairie Lotus.*
- They can remind us, as Kimberly Brubaker Bradley does in *The War that Saved My Life*, that people experiencing traumatic global events do not experience them in monolithic ways.

- They can question what is right and what is wrong given extenuating circumstances as Shūsaku Endō does in *Silence*.

With the gift of perspective comes a burden of responsibility. Creators of historical stories must ensure that developments align with the reality of the times in which they are set.[55] In doing so, they walk a fine line. If they strictly follow historical detail (say, for example, peppering dialogue with now-obsolete slang), audiences could become confused and give up. However, if creators stray too far from historical conventions in characters' speech, dress, or behavior, they could be perceived as modernizing the characters and not being faithful to history. Thus, creators of historical fiction are always balancing multiple considerations. They ponder what research has uncovered about a given time period and what average audiences will understand and accept without too much mental effort. Striking the right chord isn't always easy.

What's simpler is describing the fashions of the period and basic processes of daily life. How did people at this time bathe themselves? How did they conduct their financial affairs? How did they make bread and cheese? But this, if you will, is just the story packaging.

What's harder to pin down are the moral conventions, mental attitudes, and social customs of the day. This is an especially tricky

---

[55] At least, in theory. "Historical" romances can play fast and loose with dialogue, not to mention the thoughts and attitudes of the characters themselves.

79

business. Audiences expect characters to think and behave in relatable ways but may be unaware of just how wide a gap separates the way they think and feel from the way people did "back then." For these reasons alone, historical fiction poses a unique challenge.

It also provides unique realizations. Ones that humble me time and again. Left to myself, I tend to feel a sense of superiority just for having the "good luck" of being born now and being able to benefit from the advancements of our era. I'm tempted to look back at those who have gone before me with a specific set of assumptions about their intelligence and knowledge. Often these assumptions are rooted more in my own false sense of pride than anything else.

In historical fiction, I'm constantly conflicted. History is riddled with pain points. Particularly American history. Chattel Slavery, Jim Crow, the Indian Removal Act, the Chinese Exclusion Act—this list could go on and on. Our legacy is tarnished by our ancestors' collective sins, and we continue to grapple with the intergenerational fallout.

Still, Historical Fiction reminds me that we also benefit from our ancestors' courageous acts. This thought was driven home anew earlier this year when I watched the Sam Mendes film *1917*. These young men were slogging around in trenches, snagging their skin on barbed wire, tripping over dead horse carcasses, going hungry, and risking life and limb at every turn. The hardest thing I did today was voluntarily walk barefoot in loose, hot sand at the beach. Granted, that was just today. But still. Why do I ever complain about anything? Honestly.

Historical fiction stories offer more than just perspectives and attitude adjustments, although those are no small matters. They also provide special opportunities for spiritual reflection. In Historical Fiction, we're uniquely able to observe the interplay of immanence and transcendence.

As we noted in Chapter 2, we serve a God who is above and beyond creation—completely outside and "other"—and yet always present and near. As finite human beings, we are tightly linked to linear chronology. Our God, however, who created time as we know it, though very real and present here, is not bound to our world or our timeline. Like authors of historical fiction working outside and beyond the story, he can access a perspective we lack.

Because humans are made in his image, though, we wrestle against the mortal ties that bind us. We push and pull, seeking any means of escape. The gospel has good news in this regard. One day, we will slip that tether.

For now, engaging with Historical Fiction gives us a vague sense of what it will feel like to step outside of time, join the Savior on the other side, and mingle with saints of all ages, gaining the perspective we lack now and worshiping together before the throne of God.

In 1 Corinthians 13, Paul notes the change in perspective when transitioning from child to adult. He then contrasts this with the ultimate change in perspective that will come when we transition from here to the eternal state: "When I was a child, I spoke like a child, I thought like a child, I reasoned like a child. When I became a man, I gave up childish ways. For now we see in a mirror dimly, but then face to face. Now I know in part; then I shall know fully, even as I have been fully known."[56]

Realistic Fiction

Realistic fiction, though obviously made up, encompasses stories that could actually occur to people in believable settings. The inciting incidents might be mundane (Jason Reynolds's *Ghost*) or extreme (Laurie Halse Anderson's *Speak*); but either way, they're real-life problems. This is both a blessing and a potential curse. Audiences turn to stories to take them away from real life and forget its pressures for a while. Instead of distracting us, realistic fiction can reinforce the strain. This might explain why even critically-acclaimed TV offerings do not always fare well in the ratings (rest in peace, *Freaks and Geeks*).

Realistic fiction is generally set in the present. More often than focusing on a hero/villain dichotomy, the story tensions revolve around the trials of everyday life: identity, relational frustrations, grief, pain, confusion, disruption, disappointment, miscommunication, regret, and loss. As the audience, we find stories most relatable when the resolutions make sense and come about naturally. In realistic fiction, any hint of miracles or *deus ex machina* will have audiences rolling their eyes.

---

[56] 1 Corinthians 13:11-12.

Realistic stories rarely offer a magic wand to tidy up plots or emotions. They are, after all, attempting to stay true to life. Instead of plotlines tied in neat bows, we're given partial resolutions and messy emotions. Rather than simply entertaining us, these stories demand something, often requiring us to take hard looks at ourselves and our place in society.

A recent example would be Angie Thomas's *The Hate U Give*, originally a young adult novel and now a film by the same title. Through the eyes of the central character, Starr, we're given access to the two worlds she navigates—her neighborhood of Garden Heights, which is her cultural home, and her prestigious private school, in which she's a racial outlier. Those worlds collide when her childhood friend Khalil is fatally shot by the police. Not only must Starr bear the brunt of the emotional fallout, but she also stands at the center of larger social and cultural conflicts. Because Starr's life bridges a social divide, the story does, too. Audiences can recognize themselves not only in Starr but in a wide array of characters across the spectrum and, as a result, come to consider how they would respond in a similar situation.

Though some people bypass realistic fiction in favor of formulaic plots and the promise of happily-ever-after endings, realistic stories carry great value. They help us view the world through perspectives other than our own. I've not yet been elderly, but I've read Marilynne Robin's *Gilead* and sympathized with Reverend Ames as he watches the light move across the floor and contemplates his own mortality. I haven't wrestled with cultural identity or wondered how I fit into dominant American society, but I've read Tommy Orange's *There, There* and sympathized with Jacquie Red Feather, eleven days sober and more at home in a car than a house. I've never lived in a football town, but I've watched *Friday Night Lights* and observed how the pressures affected Coach Taylor, his family, the players, and the surrounding community.

When we create and consume realistic fiction, we are reminded of the direct example and explicit call of our Savior, Jesus Christ. As God incarnate, he entered the human experience and walked among us. As the God-man, he understands our sorrows and sufferings—and not just because we take them to him in prayer. He empathizes with human weakness because he's been human himself. He hasn't just observed the human condition—he's lived inside our perspective. Therefore, one reason we can hold on in the midst of trial and tribulation is the very nature of Jesus himself.

> Since then we have a great high priest who has passed through the heavens, Jesus, the Son of God, let us hold fast our confession. For we do not have a high priest who is unable to sympathize with our weaknesses, but one who in every respect has been tempted as we are, yet without sin. Let us then with confidence draw near to the throne of grace, that we may receive mercy and find grace to help in time of need.[57]

---

[57] Hebrews 4:14-15.

As a follower of Jesus, Paul directly modeled this behavior.

> For though I am free from all, I have made myself a servant to all, that I might win more of them. To the Jews I became as a Jew, in order to win Jews. To those under the law I became as one under the law (though not being myself under the law) that I might win those under the law. To those outside the law I became as one outside the law (not being outside the law of God but under the law of Christ) that I might win those outside the law. To the weak I became weak, that I might win the weak. I have become all things to all people, that by all means I might save some. I do it all for the sake of the gospel, that I may share with them in its blessings.[58]

In order to share the gospel with as many people as possible while avoiding needless offense, Paul "demonstrated his willingness to enter into other people's lives and share their circumstances. He did everything for the sake of the gospel and from a desire to be a partner in the blessings it brings."[59]

Of course, we are limited. We cannot literally experience everything ourselves. But wide engagement with realistic fiction stories can help bridge the experience gap. Am I arguing that every time you're watching TV or going to the movies or listening to a podcast or reading

---

[58] I Corinthians 9:19-23.
[59] Dachollom Datiri, "1 Corinthians," in *Africa Bible Commentary*, ed. Tokunboh Adeyemo (Grand Rapids: Zondervan, 2006), 1414.

a book, you're doing so *for the sake of the gospel*? Of course not. Consuming stories is not enough to fulfill the Great Commission.

Through engaging with Realistic Fiction, we can ask our Creator to increase our empathy, particularly with people whose experiences differ from our own. That way when we meet people whose experiences mirror those about which we've only read, we'll at least have a small level of insight that will facilitate becoming all things to all people, that by all means we might save some. At the very least, perhaps we will ask fewer silly questions.

Broadening our intake of Realistic Fiction, to the extent that it leads to empathy, helps us reflect our Savior and could possibly contribute to a more effective witness. Empathy becomes a channel through which we pour out the love of God in the way we demonstrate and proclaim his love.

Comedy

Whether slapstick, deadpan, wry, or screwball, one purpose of comedy is to provoke laughter. In finding what makes us laugh, comic storytellers delve deeply into what makes us human and how we process our lives. Though there can definitely be a dark side to comedy (satire and black humor being notable examples[60]), for the most part, comic stories uncover the humor in everyday situations. In its most shallow

---

[60] Think Jonathan Swift's 1729 essay "A Modest Proposal" or the 2008 headline "Wealthy Teen Nearly Experiences Consequence" courtesy of *The Onion*. Both point to problematic situations and highlight deeper surrounding social issues.

forms, comedy merely amuses; at the height of its powers, it educates, informs, and restores.

Comedy works best when it plays on situations we recognize, know well, and have lived through ourselves. One of the main tenants of comedy-writing is to know your audience; that's because at its core, comedy is about human connection.[61] Comic stories invite us to come together and commiserate over the wonder and wretchedness of being a person. To scratch our heads over people and scenarios that baffle us (NBC's *The Office*), to shake our heads at the ridiculousness of everyday life (David Sedaris's *When You Are Engulfed in Flames*), or to look back at things that once made us cry but now we can laugh at with others (*The Mortified Podcast*). All of these aspects are on full display in live comedy. Though stand-up has a reputation for crass jokes and ribaldry, stand-up comedians often take audiences on emotional journeys equal parts insight and punchlines (Mike Birbiglia's *What I Should Have Said Was Nothing: Tales from My Secret Public Journal*).

Of course, if a rule of comedy is to know your audience and write jokes that will land with them, it follows that the comedy appealing to the dominant culture will tend to get the most airtime. It's a predicament comedy writer Mindy Kaling has wrestled with since her breakthrough. Though she got her start writing for *The Office*, Kaling has since started telling stories reflecting her experiences as an Indian-

---

[61] Mary O'Hara, "How Comedy Makes Us Better People," *BBC*, https://www.bbc.com/future/article/20160829-how-laughter-makes-us-better-people (accessed April 4, 2020).

American. As of this writing, her freshest offering, the Netflix series *Never Have I Ever*, tells the coming-of-age story of an Indian-American teenage girl named Devi.

> "For all of us in the writers' room, particularly those of us who were the children of immigrants, which comprised most of my staff, it was about sharing those stories of feeling 'other,'" said Kaling, who is also a first-generation Indian-American. "One of the best parts about being in that room was realizing that they felt so many of the same things I did, and it was such a relief. It made me feel like, 'OK, I'm, like, normal.'"[62]

In writing comedy rooted in the Indian-American community, Kaling is seeking more than simply a few shared laughs. (Though laughing together is certainly not nothing.) She's also making sense of her own experiences and connecting them with others, both within the Indian-American community and beyond.

Consumers of comedy need not share the *exact* experience featured. We can all agree some comic set-ups are a bit outlandish—particularly in romantic comedies! But we're often able to identify with the emotional journeys the central figures go through. We can share a laugh over these things because humor is intrinsic to human nature. And it's intrinsic to human nature because it's intrinsic to our Creator's.

---

[62] Priya Arora, "Mindy Kaling's Netflix Show Tells a New Kind of Story: One Like Hers," *The New York Times,* https://www.nytimes.com/2020/04/27/arts/television/mindy-kaling-never-have-I-ever-netflix.html (accessed May 26, 2020).

Yes, God has a healthy sense of humor. In Scripture, we see the Creator delighting in animals as they play, laughing over ironic situations, and—in the person and work of Jesus, sparking humor through comic understatement and even puns.[63] The nature of God's sense of humor, and the implications for the everyday life of the Christian, feels more or less overlooked in the theological circles where I travel. In my opinion, this is a harmful oversight.

If every good and perfect gift does indeed come from above, as Brother James writes in his epistle, then humor is also a gift from above.[64] Like other divine favors, it should be celebrated as such and stewarded as a responsibility.

All human beings are formed in God's image and therefore bear the capacity of reflecting him—that includes a sense of humor. We may display this attribute imperfectly. In our fallen state, we can abuse it. Still, those of us who claim the title *Christian* represent our Creator poorly if we fail to nurture this attribute.

Discussion Questions:

---

[63] Though not quoted directly here, my thoughts on this section were influenced by an article that appeared in the 1982 edition of *The Asbury Seminarian*. I'm not certain I'm on board with all its assertions, but the author makes some wonderful points about our God's sense of humor and some possible implications. For more, see Fred D. Layman, "Theology and Humor," *The Asbury Seminarian: Vol. 38: No. 1, p. 3-25.* Available at: *https://place.asburyseminary.edu/asburyjournal/vol38/iss1/2* (accessed April 4, 2020).

[64] James 1:17.

1. Of the four genres discussed in this chapter, which ones tend to draw you in the most and keep you coming back for more? Why do you think that is?

   _____

   _____

   _____

2. What spiritual connections from this chapter caught your attention?

   _____

   _____

   _____

3. Can you think of some Scriptural examples of God expressing his sense of humor?

   _____

   _____

   _____

4. What further spiritual parallels can you draw from stories in these genres?

   a. Drama

_____

_____

_____

b. Historical Fiction

_____

_____

_____

c. Realistic Fiction

_____

_____

_____

d. Comedy

_____

_____

_____

Notes

_____

_____

_____

_____

_____

_____

_____

_____

_____

_____

_____

_____

_____

_____

_____

_____

_____

_____

_____

_____

_____

_____

_____

_____

Chapter 6

|

The last two chapters focused on how fictional narratives can connect directly to the truths of the gospel. In this chapter, we will examine several non-fiction genres in a similar light. We'll observe key staples of each type and consider how they can connect us to universal truths and the hope of Christ.

Biography, Autobiography, and Memoir

Biographies, autobiographies, and memoirs—these three styles provide a zoomed-in focus on real, non-fiction lives. In visual media, they may take the forms of biopics and documentaries. In podcasts, they might form a single episode or encompass an entire season or series. The stories they tell run the gamut from inspirational (Tom Hooper's *The King's Speech*) to heroic (Kasi Lemmons's *Harriet*), to thought-provoking (Sean Penn's *Into the Wild*), to blatantly revisionist (Michael Gracey's *The Greatest Showman*) to downright baffling (Angie Martinez's *Infamous: The Tekashi 6ix9ine Story*). More often than movies, documentaries, or podcasts, however, life stories have been detailed in books.

While a biography is researched and presented by a separate author, autobiographies and memoirs are written by the subjects themselves. The lines between them are thin but clear. While biographies and autobiographies are more focused on timelines and events, memoirs are more reflective and detail emotional developments.

Self-penned life stories can be written by the very famous (Michelle Obama's *Becoming*) or by relative nobodies (David Crow's *The Pale-Faced Lie*). They could be hilarious (Trevor Noah's *Born a Crime*) or heartbreaking (Rachael Denhollander's *What Is a Girl Worth?*).

If a subject writes her own story, she's able to offer key insights and inside scoops. She can provide context not available to an outsider no matter how much research he does (Edwidge Danticat in *Brother, I'm Dying*). However, by telling her own story, she may lack the objectivity needed to make sense of her situation (Pearl S. Buck in *My Several Worlds*). While it may feel uncomfortable to surrender our story to an outside voice, often an outside perspective does wonders for framing a single life experience within a larger context (as Zora Neale Hurston does for Cudjo Lewis in *Barracoon*.)[65]

A favorite biographical subset of mine is the spiritual biography. These books detail a subject's faith journey. This may encompass a move toward conversion (Carolyn Weber's *Surprised by Oxford*) or deconversion (Tara Westover's *Educated*). Reading as a Christian, I always interpret someone's spiritual progression through that specific lens. This introduces a specific dynamic. Though spiritual biographies can feel frustrating and make for some painful reading at times, they also offer critical insight into the different ways people can experience faith. Spiritual biographies can be just as enlightening whether the

---

[65] Most of us will never have to worry about this. Either we fly so far under the radar that nobody would bother or we're already dead by the time the book's written. By that time, it's no longer our concern.

subject shares your faith perspective or not! There's a reason for this—one that undergirds how we process other people's narratives.

When we immerse ourselves in true-life stories, we're accomplishing several things simultaneously. First, we're observing the world, our lives, and our place in it. Second, we're looking for meaning, particularly in tragedies. Third, we're seeking to hone our perceptions of people. We're hoping to create real-life archetypes, propping them up either as heroes to be emulated or villains to be reviled. We're seeking inspiration from the former and cataloging warning signs from the latter.

Either way, we're drawn to people's stories because we crave wisdom, reassurance, and connection. We discover wisdom as we learn from the lives of others—both their successes and failures. We find reassurance in the story's conclusions, most of which imply something good comes of it in the end. We forge connections when we recognize our own thoughts and experiences on the page. We recognize that we're not alone—others have lived these struggles, felt these emotions, or pondered these same questions. Few things in life are more reassuring than moments when we suspect that maybe we're not the weird ones after all!

We feel these emotions so deeply because of our nature. If you read the creation account in Genesis, you'll see that from the beginning, humans were intended for meaningful connections. God created us to be in relationship with him and with each other. Made in the image of a

Triune God, we are incomplete without it. Ideally, we would all be rightly connected with the God who made us, with the body of Christ, and with greater society. True life stories remind us of why these connections matter, what they look like when they're working well, and the damage caused when they do not.

Narrative Nonfiction

Narrative Nonfiction is what you get when an author details a real-life event with all the literary powers of novel-writing. In the publishing world, this genre is sometimes called Creative Nonfiction or Literary Nonfiction. The events are factual, but the style is so dramatic and lively that audiences get sucked right in.

Narrative nonfiction stories are often based in history. They may focus on greater societal issues (David Grann's *Killers of the Flower Moon*) or on highly localized events (Wesley Lowery's *They Can't Kill Us All*). They may detail shared triumphs (Daniel James Brown's *The Boys in the Boat*) or communal tragedies (Kate Moore's *Radium Girls*). The purpose of these accounts is not merely to convey events the same way a history textbook or a newspaper article might. Instead, they ignite the imagination. They draw us into the worlds of the central characters, reminding us that these are not simply names on a page but living, breathing people swept up in dramatic events, often not of their making and beyond their control.

In some ways, reading narrative nonfiction reminds me of reading Holy Scriptures. Not that both are somehow inspired or authoritative in the same way. But in dramatic, real-life accounts, we're reminded that God works in and through the lives of real, actual people. Some are not even aware that God's the one at work. But he is. Those of us outside the story can see it even when they can't.

Scripture teems with real, messy people who are struggling and confused, alternately failing and triumphing amid real problems. Though we can read their entire life stories in a few chapters (sometimes in a single verse!), these people lived day by day, not knowing how anything would turn out. They're flawed, fallen, and flailing, caught up in large-scale events.

Mary and Martha, loving and serving alongside Jesus—but also bickering. David singled out as a man after God's own heart—but committing sexual sin and murder. Abraham demonstrating remarkable faith in his call to follow God to an unknown land—later surrendering to fear and asking Sarah to lie for him. Peter squabbling with Jesus. Jesus himself crying in Gethsemane, wrestling with the Father's will.

When we read Scripture, we not only see humanity in full, messy display; but we also witness the glory of Yahweh, a God who does not need humans to be anything other than what they are. He can accomplish his purposes either way, with or without us. If he can speak through a donkey, he can speak through anyone.[66]

---

[66] Which is good news for us because we've all behaved like jackasses at some point. Numbers 22:21-30.

The parallels between the Bible and Narrative Nonfiction aren't total. Apart from the question of inspiration, there is the question of purpose. The Scriptures were written for our learning, yes; but they were also written for our comfort and hope.[67] Part of that comfort and hope comes from observing the life narratives recorded in its pages. But the greater share of our comfort is administered directly by our one true Comforter. Throughout the process of reading and meditating on Scripture, the Holy Spirit is at work, teaching us, guiding us in all truth, and bearing witness with our spirit that we are children of God.[68]

True Crime

As the genre name indicates, True Crime stories explore actual criminal events. In general, they dissect the lead-up to the crime and unpack the surrounding mystery. They contextualize the major players and document the fallout. Some True Crime writers sensationalize high-profile crimes, while others shine a light on obscure cases that would otherwise have slipped under the radar. In many cases, the public would never have learned the victims' names if not for a book, movie, show, or podcast.

True Crime stories fill the spectrum from bone-chilling (Ann Rule's *Stranger Beside Me*), to cautionary (Christopher Goffard's *Dirty John*), to borderline farcical (Eric Goode and Rebekah Chaiklin's *Tiger King*). The purpose may be to settle guilt once and for all (HBO's *The*

---

[67] Romans 15:4.
[68] Romans 8:16.

Jinx), shine a light on cold cases (Ryan White's *The Keepers*), or call into question previously settled verdicts (Sarah Koenig's *Serial*, Season 1). The narrative focus may land on crimes against specific individuals (Skye Borgman's *Abducted in Plain Sight*) or underscore collective patterns of criminality disproportionately affecting certain segments of society (Laura Paglin's *Unseen*).

According to experts who track this sort of thing, the True Crime genre has seen an uptick in popularity in recent years, correlating with the rise of podcasts.[69] Writing for *Rolling Stone*, Michael Stahl asserts that podcasts and True Crime seem made for each other. Accounting for this, he cites factors such as forced intimacy (the show host speaking directly into your ear) and mood-inducing audio elements. He also points out that audio-consumed true crime offers listeners a danger-free adrenaline rush from the comfort of their own couches. Stahl further notes that "crimes themselves happen in a serialized manner, one action followed by another and then another. Therefore, serialized storytelling can capture the timeline of a crime in a unique, frighteningly accurate way."[70]

---

[69] As of August of 2019, true crime podcasts accounted for 50% of the top ten podcasts on iTunes. For more on this, see Katie Heaney, "Is True Crime Over?" *The Cut*, https://www.thecut.com/2019/08/is-true-crime-over.html (accessed April 9, 2020).

[70] Michael Stahl, "Why True Crime and Podcasts Were Made For Each Other," *RollingStone.com*, https://www.rollingstone.com/culture/culture-features/why-true-crime-and-podcasts-were-made-for-each-other-128984/ (accessed April 9, 2020).

I can attest to this. When I was training for a marathon in 2018, I would binge listen to True Crime podcasts on long runs.[71] Not only did they actually take my mind off how far I was running, but they would also suck me so far and so completely into the story that I can still remember where I was along my running route when certain twists dropped.

I have a love-hate relationship with True Crime. While the bone-deep realness carries a unique intensity, those very same qualities terrify me. I'm a single woman of small stature who spends a lot of time alone. I don't need extra disaster narratives writing themselves in the back of my mind as I bumble through life. Add to that the general discomfort I feel over how these stories are often sensationalized and exploited, and I question the wisdom of engaging my attention too heavily in this area.

Still, these are real things that happen to real people in the real world. It feels wrong to look away. I have friends who have been abducted, whose parents are murderers, who have lost siblings to tragedy, who have escaped abuse. To ignore True Crime would be to ignore resources that could help me understand what they've been through and how they're uniquely affected.

People gravitate to True Crime through a variety of motivations. Some are fascinated by the extremes of good and evil and want to know

---

[71] I can also attest that a heavy diet of True Crime can warp your perceptions, causing you to sense crime everywhere—even in innocuous situations. I will expound more on this in my forthcoming book *Socially Awkward*, due for release in 2021.

what makes criminals tick.[72] Others, particularly women, identify with the victims and hope to learn tips and tricks to escape such fates themselves.[73] And yes, some are drawn to the lurid and grisly details. Most of us probably approach the genre with mixed motives.

When I engage with True Crime stories, I'm reminded of three undeniable biblical truths. First, the human heart is capable of great evil. Second, we're not always good at spotting the "bad guys" in our lives. Anyone is capable of anything, and even the "unlikely" commit horrible crimes. Third, crimes and disasters don't just happen to others. They don't just happen to people *like* us, either. They can happen *to us.*

What strikes me after having spent my share of time in this genre is that nearly every True Crime story starts the same way. The days on which serious crimes occur start out "as any other day." Interviewees often underscore how otherwise banal the moments before the crime were. People wake up, make lists and plans, throw laundry in the washer, and back the car down the driveway headed to the store. Until disaster strikes, it's just another day.

We don't like to think about it, but that's so real. We don't know when any of us or our loved ones will walk out the front door for the

---

[72]Max Darrow, "SPECIAL REPORT: What's Behind the Fascination with True Crime Stories?" *News3lv.com*, https://news3lv.com/news/local/special-report-whats-behind-the-fascination-with-true-crime-stories (accessed April 8, 2020).
[73]Clare Thorp, "Why Are We Obsessed with True Crime?" *The Telegraph*, https://www.telegraph.co.uk/tv/a-confession/why-do-we-love-true-crime/ (accessed April 8, 2020).

last time. Along these lines, the New Testament writer James reminds us of the fleeting nature of daily life.

> Come now, you who say, "Today or tomorrow we will go into such and such a town and spend a year there and trade and make a profit"—yet you do not know what tomorrow will bring. What is your life? For you are a mist that appears for a little time and then vanishes. Instead you ought to say, "If the Lord wills, we will live and do this or that." As it is, you boast in your arrogance.[74]

None of us know how much time we will have on this earth with our friends, family, and loved ones. We have no guarantee that they will not be taken from us one day—or that we will be taken from them. Any day could bring reversals, tragedies, and disasters.

It is arrogant to believe that we have absolute control over our plans, our days, and our lives. It is foolish to allow these moments to slip through our fingers, never considering that each one could be our last. We must, as the Psalmist reminds us, learn to number our days and thereby gain a heart of wisdom.[75] True Crime reminds us of this.

Discussion Questions:

---

[74] James 4:13-16a.
[75] Psalm 90:12.

1. Of the five genres discussed in this chapter, which ones tend to draw you in the most and keep you coming back for more? Why do you think that is?

    _____

    _____

    _____

2. What spiritual connections from this chapter captured your attention?

    _____

    _____

    _____

3. What further spiritual parallels can you draw from stories in these genres?

    a. Biography

    _____

    _____

    _____

    b. Autobiography

    _____

    _____

    _____

c. Memoir

_____

_____

_____

d. Narrative Nonfiction

_____

_____

_____

e. True Crime

_____

_____

_____

Notes

PART III

Chapter 7

|

No matter what type of stories we enjoy, a few common themes found across genres further reflect deep spiritual truths. Some do so wittingly, some unwittingly. One of those themes is near and dear to all our hearts. Relationships. Though we briefly brushed against this concept in a previous chapter, we will take time here to unfold a few specific aspects in need of direct attention.

Built for It

From the beginning of time, humans were built for relationships. Relationships are fundamental to our nature because they are fundamental to the God who made us. Our Triune God created *out of relationship.*

Read Genesis 1, and you will discover every member of the Godhead present and active in forming the cosmos. The Spirit hovered, and the Father spoke, creating not just *with words* but through *the Word.* John details this dynamic in the opening of his Gospel.

In the beginning was the Word, and *the Word was with God, and the Word was God.* He was in the beginning with God. *All things were made through him,* and *without him was not any thing made that was made.* In him was life, and the life was the light of men. The light shines in the darkness, and the darkness has not overcome it…The true light, which gives light to everyone, was coming into the world. *He was in the world, and the world was made through him, yet the world did not know him.* He came to his own, and his own people did not receive him. But to all who did receive him, who believed in his name, he gave the right to become children of God, who were born, not of blood nor of the will of the flesh nor of the will of man, but of God. *And the Word became flesh and dwelt among us, and we have seen his glory, glory as of the only Son from the Father, full of grace and truth.*[76]

When we discuss being made in God's image, we must not lose sight of this fundamental truth. The Godhead, as Trinity, has always existed in full and complete relationship. Tim Keller underscores the importance of understanding this dynamic: "If this is ultimate reality, if this is what the God who made the universe is like, then this truth bristles and explodes with life-shaping, glorious implications for us. *If this world was made by a triune God, relationships of love are what life is really all about.*"[77]

When we come to faith in Christ, we enter the divine dance with the Trinity.[78] But though God exists naturally as the Three-in-One, we are only one. We are not self-existent and self-sustaining. In God's plan, we need him and need each other. We are meant to thrive in relationships.

---

[76] John 1:1-14, emphasis mine.
[77] Timothy Keller, *Jesus the King: Understanding the Life and Death of the Son of God* (New York: Penguin Books, 2016), 9.
[78] Ibid, 11.

The Thing about Relationships

Here in America in the year of our Lord 2020 (which is when I'm writing this), the word *relationship* carries heavy romantic connotations. Think about how we use the word in casual conversation to see that we generally do the same thing. "Are you in a relationship?" we ask, as if we don't have to specify which type of relationship we mean, which we don't. Type the word *relationship* into Google and tell me what sorts of articles fill the first page of results. I did this, and all but one of them were clearly designed to target the reader's love life. The way the word is used seems to imply that romantic relationships trump all others (which is a cultural thread we could spend quite some time pulling; however, since that is not really my point, let's move on).

We begin our lives in relationship to another, supported by our mothers in utero. We then maintain a significant number of important relationships throughout our lives. Family member and friend, neighbor and fellow citizen, coworker and colleague, sister and brother in the Body of Christ—all these bonds play a critical role in our development and ongoing wellbeing.

Writing in the seventeenth century, Christian poet John Donne offered powerful imagery depicting the interconnectedness of all humankind: "No man is an island entire unto itself. Every person is a piece of the continent, a part of the mainland. If a clod is washed away by the sea, Europe is diminished, just as if the sea had washed away a mountain or one of your friend's grand houses. A person's death diminishes me, because I am involved in humankind."[79]

Donne's point is that all humanity is so interconnected that to lose one person is to diminish us all. Christians would do well to take this to heart. Jesus taught that we could only thrive in connection to him ("I am the vine; you are the branches"); and that church members thrive when they stay connected to one another ("one body with many members").[80]

I've become known for saying that in God's plan we all need each other, and that's true. What I haven't articulated as often is why. We need each other because though we're made in God's image, we are not gods ourselves. We are neither self-existent nor self-sufficient. Sometimes we see weaknesses as results of the curse. But as Jen Wilkin reminds us in her book *None Like Him*, Adam and Eve demonstrated needs even before the Fall.

> God created them needy, that in their need they might turn to the Source of all that is needful, acknowledge their need, and worship. Instead, they angled for autonomy. Like them, we see human need as a flaw and human self-sufficiency as a crowning achievement. We become plate-spinners and ball-jugglers. With

---

[79] Which he follows up with the wonderfully morbid, "Therefore, never send to know for whom the bell tolls; it tolls for you." For more, see John Donne, "Meditation XVII" in *Religious Poetry and Prose*, ed. Henry L. Carrigan, Jr. (Brewster, MA: Paraclete Press, 1999), 91.

[80] John 15:5; 1 Corinthians 12:12.

our lives collapsing around us, we paint on a smile and fake our way through another Sunday at church, denying our need for authenticity…God, in his ultimate wisdom, created us to need him. And he also created us to need each other…Satisfaction is the process of learning increasing dependence, not autonomy.[81] Expressing need is not a failing but a natural expression of human nature. We are built for, birthed out of, and destined to live in relationship, both to our Creator and fellow created beings.

Given their fundamental importance in the human experience, relationships naturally play an outsized role in the stories we tell. One American TV show that exemplifies the multifaceted natures of human relationships is NBC's *Parks and Recreation.*

My Swan(son) Song

Parks and Rec isn't everyone's favorite comedy, and I get that. The first season doesn't exactly inspire confidence. Even I skip it when I do a series re-watch. Still, the writing does something with relationships that I simply adore—particularly in the later seasons.

First, though there are romantic and family relationships highlighted along the way, the story centers friendships. There's the friendship between dedicated public servant Leslie Knope and nurse Ann Perkins, of course, which gets a lot of attention; however, the primary relationship of the show is between Leslie and her boss in the

[81] Jen Wilkin, *None Like Him: 10 Ways God Is Different from Us (and Why That's a Good Thing)* (Wheaton: Crossway, 2016), 62-63.

Parks and Recreation Department, Ron Swanson. (More on this pairing later.)

In truth, however, Leslie develops meaningful friendships with every member of her team; and though she's initially the glue holding them all together, she doesn't keep that role forever. At some point, each character also develops relational bond with one another. As they grow in their relationships, they grow in their support for one another. Think Tom and Donna taking a depressed Ben with them on their Treat Yo' Self outing; April giving Chris a movie ticket when he's lonely; Ron offering to pay for Andy's college classes. If you haven't seen the show, know that each example just given shows the tender and delicate threads of friendship binding these characters increasingly tighter and closer.

Particularly in Leslie's relationships, though, we observe connections that are real, genuine, and multi-faceted. With Leslie and Ann, we see women who don't sideline their attachment when romantic partners come along. With Donna, we see a bond that can safely express grievances and survive instances of mutual frustration. With Ben, we see that friendship between men and women can serve as a strong foundation for romantic love; with Ron, we see that it doesn't necessarily have to.

To be honest, the friendship between Leslie and Ron is one of my favorite aspects of the show. We see a deep commitment based on mutual respect between a woman and a man who are not romantically attracted to one another. Their connection benefits not just them but also those around them.

Case Study: Leslie and Ron

Leslie Knope and Ron Swanson are a perfect example of what it looks like to disagree strongly on principle while maintaining a charitable and respectful relationship.[82] They show us not only that you *can* love people you strongly disagree with but that you *should*. For their sake, your sake, and the sake of your community.

If you're familiar with the show, you'll remember that Ron and Leslie did not get along well at first. In fact, the show eventually reveals that when she first joined the department, he attempted to fire her multiple times. Eventually, they develop a mutual respect and close friendship.

Ron was won to friendship not because he and Leslie eventually came to see eye-to-eye but because she relentlessly invested in their relationship. Though they were often ideologically at odds, their constant friction, instead of creating chaos, actually benefited the whole group. Time and again, their steady stream of arguments and counterbalancing kept them both from veering into the worst extremes of their own positions.

---

[82] I hashed out an early version of these thoughts in a Twitter thread on May 21, 2019. Read the original posts here: https://twitter.com/RuthMBuchanan/status/1130854827552935936 (accessed March 26, 2020).

In the latter seasons of the show, nobody needed a counterbalance quite as badly as obnoxious city council member Jeremy Jamm. As terrible as Jamm was to deal with (so terrible), it's clear that being around the group—particularly around Leslie—casts a vision for friendship in his imagination and makes him long for it himself.

When Jamm is at his lowest, though Leslie and Ron are temporarily at odds with one another, they both step in to save him. They become a team to fight a common enemy (Tammy 2) for the good of someone who was, at one time, also their enemy (Jamm).

This is why, while there are certainly times to distance ourselves from certain people, we shouldn't jump to block, mute, and cancel everyone who disagrees. First, we all need a Ron to our Leslie and a Leslie to our Ron. Others need it too. They need us to counterbalance one another, and they need us to serve as bastions of friendship and sanity in a world run relationally amok. Second, if society can't look to the people of God to act as ministers of reconciliation, where can they look?

Theoretically, followers of Christ are in the best position to show the world what it looks like to live in right relationships, particularly with those who are not like us or with whom we've had disagreements in the past. Repentance, reconciliation, restitution, and restoration are essential facets of Christian engagement—both on the small interpersonal scale and the grand social scale.

These steps aren't easy, but they're possible for two reasons: First, Christ paved the way and left us an example. Second, the Holy Spirit lives in us, lending us the same power that raised Jesus from the dead.

Maintaining relationships characterized by repentance, reconciliation, restitution, and restoration is not easy, but it's possible and worth it—for our own good and the good of our community.

The Jerry Problem

Given *Parks and Rec*'s otherwise kind-spirited nature, its treatment of Jerry Gergich is a bit of a headscratcher. Jerry is a true gem, gentle and kind—though a bit hapless. Yet for nearly the entirety of the show's run, he's treated horribly by his co-workers. Despite being upbeat, helpful, and unproblematic, Jerry is almost universally despised.

The writing choices here are interesting. Irony creates strong humor, of course, and there's always something funny about ironic and irrational annoyance. And there's something to be said for the popularity of this storytelling technique. *Parks and Recreation* isn't the only sitcom to have a mild-mannered, kind-spirited character who everyone inexplicably hates. Think Toby in *The Office* or Terence in *Kim's Convenience*.

Still, it seems an odd writing choice for a show that otherwise hit friendship notes so sweetly. If you watch the show all the way to its last season, you'll learn (spoiler alert!) that things do shift for him. Jerry eventually becomes the mayor of Pawnee and adored by the town.

What are we, the viewers, to make of Jerry's "redemption" arc? Writing for *The Atlantic,* cultural observer and critic Megan Garber offers this.

> Ron once described Jerry as someone who "shrivels up when you shine a light on him." What Jerry's seven-season arc suggested, though, was the opposite: that while he may hide in plain sight, he is well worth the effort to discover. Jerry started out on Parks and Rec as a familiar stranger, the guy who is there but not there—the guy you know, but don't really know. And he ends the show as the mayor of Pawnee. He ends the show, in other words, validated and vindicated. He ends the show soaring. In that sense, Jerry is a hopeful stand-in for all the people who have talents and values that aren't recognized by others—all the people who are unseen or ignored because they're the wrong color or gender or size or clique. He is a reminder of all the potential contributions that are quashed through such failures of vision. We are all, basically, Jerry…we will all, at some point, be loved—both despite, and because of, who we really are.[83]

I don't know if I'm fully on board with her take. For one thing, seeing ourselves as the Jerry of our own timelines lets us off too easy. There will always be people who don't like us, and sometimes their dislike is warranted. But there's another problem with this perspective. At one

---

[83] Megan Garber, "And the Meek Shall Inherit Pawnee," *The Atlantic*, https://www.theatlantic.com/entertainment/archive/2015/02/and-the-meek-shall-inherit-pawnee/385985/ (accessed March 28, 2020).

point or another, we've been on the *giving* end of unwarranted mockery, loathing, and criticism.

If the show wants us to see ourselves in Jerry and recognize that we are all secret heroes, it's undercut by the fact that the majority of Jerry's redemption arc happens offscreen. We see him become mayor, yes, but even his mayor-ship is initially a joke; and though his time in office does become significant later down the line, we're shown this only in retrospect. Jerry's vindication isn't significant enough to be shown. Perhaps that's supposed to be part of the joke—a deepening of the irony. In my opinion, it's just a further complication in the Jerry Problem.

Solving Our Jerry Problems

I don't know if we can solve The Jerry Problem as it appears in the writing choices of *Parks and Rec*. We're much better off saving our energy for solving our own relational issues. We all have them. I know I do.

Each of our interpersonal issues is complex and multifaceted, and sometimes wrestling through them feels like too much work. The only way you'll keep your head in the game is by tapping in to the right motivation.

When you want to give up on relationships, remember your origins. You were created by a relational God, and his nature is reflected in yours. As it's worded in the Westminster Shorter Catechism, "Man's chief end is to glorify God, and *to enjoy him forever.*"[84] Enjoying a relationship with God humbles us and better positions us to live in relationship with others. Relationships are foundational to human flourishing and are therefore worth investing in, working through, and fighting for. Not just for our own sake, but for the sake of our communities and, by extension, the world.

Relationships are also worth reflecting accurately on page and on screen. Those of us who are culture makers (writers, filmmakers, playwrights, poets, songwriters, and storytellers of every stripe) bear a special responsibility here. In addition to living in right relationships, we must ensure that the stories we tell, whether explicitly or implicitly, reflect the absolute truth about God, humankind, and how we are to live in relationship with one another.

Discussion Questions:

1. Discuss the contemporary use of the word *relationship*. Do you agree with the assertion that in our current American social imagination, this word carries romantic connotations? If so, what might this reveal about our society?

_____

_____

_____

---

[84] Westminster Project, http://www.shortercatechism.com/ (accessed June 11, 2020). Emphasis mine.

2. What proofs do you see of our deep human need for relationships? What might this reveal about God, others, and ourselves?

_____

_____

_____

3. What stories have you taken in recently that accurately depict truths of human relationships? Can you think of any that falls short in this area?

_____

_____

_____

4. How can understanding our basic need for relationships impact the stories we tell and how we receive them?

_____

_____

_____

Notes

_____

_____

_____

_____

_____

_____

_____

_____

_____

_____

_____

_____

_____

_____

_____

_____

_____

_____

_____

_____

Chapter 8

A few years ago, I was with my niece at the library. She was around seven at the time. She picked out her books first and had to wait for me to finish up. She'd already started a book and couldn't put it down long enough even to walk to the self-checkout. She walked along beside me, paperback practically glued to her face, while I steered her around corners. It was a thin chapter book, the formulaic serialized style kids that age gobble right up.

"How's the book?" I asked.

"I can't wait to finish it."

"Why?"

"It's going to have a happy ending!"

I steered us toward the checkout. "How do you know?"

Her head swiveled toward me. She scrunched up her face in awe at my stupidity. "They all do!"

Happy Endings

In my teen years, I loved the Christian Fiction genre, particularly World War II sagas and pioneer romances. The gooier the better. I could not slurp them up fast enough. Beautiful women in silk dresses and the handsome, rough-hewn men who loved them. "Fallen" bad boys restored by the gentle care of a godly woman. Wounded veterans who, though blinded in battle, learn to see with eyes of faith. That sort of thing. Most stories held to this underlying ethos: though there were

121

pains and regrets and rocks along the path, there was always a sunset at the end of the trail. God causes all things to work together for good, generally in 250 pages.

From a storytelling perspective, I found comfort in a sure thing. I liked knowing what was coming and resting assured that by the end of the book, I would get exactly what I was paying for. This was especially important because I funded my book purchases with the same meagre fast food paychecks funding my college account. I couldn't afford to risk my precious $4.25/hour on a book that might be a dud.

Then I hit adulthood full-stride. I had some heartbreak in the rearview mirror. Now that I had a few miles on me, a non-stop parade of happily ever afters no longer rang true. Had it ever been true? Scripture does say that all things work together for the good to those who love God and are called according to his purpose.[85] But what did "all things working together for good" look like in a life like mine?

"HEA Only"

In my early days trying to publish, I read submission guidelines on a staggering number of websites. Along the way, I learned a bit of industry shorthand. I was submitting women's fiction at the time, and I kept seeing the term *HEA Only*. This meant the agent or publisher in question would only consider stories that ended "Happily Ever After." Another term I encountered was HFN, which stands for "Happy For Now." In Happy For Now, all story conflicts aren't resolved, but the

---

[85] Romans 8:28.

characters reach a level of peace and contentment within their ongoing difficulties.

Both these ending styles have their place, and sticking to one or the other makes sense. Brands thrive when they develop a product that consumers love, and they stick to producing it. We love HFN because it reflects the way most of our lives go: happy interludes during which ongoing conflicts recede into the background. We love HEA because we like to imagine life works that way—that all problems can be resolved, relationships mended, and spiritual wounds healed. Like my niece, I wish all stories, on and off the page, ended happily. Sometimes, though, a happy ending (be it HEA or HFN) is less about what truly *happens* but about where we place the ending.

Where to End the Story

In storytelling, we're able to give almost any story an HEA or HFN for this simple reason: we decide where to put the ending. If I were to novelize the story of a real-life couple I know, I could easily frame it multiple ways. If I wanted to, I could make it a romantic Happily Ever After or a realistic Happy For Now. To make it HEA, I would end the story when they elope during WWII. So romantic! Behold the triumph of love in a dark time. However, if I wanted to frame their story more realistically, I would continue to their eventual divorce, years of estrangement, and, only very late in life, their partial reconciliation. The type of story depends on where I place the ending.

Of course, in real life there are no HEA's or HFN's. We live through our highs and lows, but we don't get to tie off the edges of our stories during our happiest moments. Our plotlines keep moving without our permission, fraying and knotting and unraveling in ways we could not have predicted. That's because we're not the authors of our own stories. We live *within* our stories, not outside them. Only the Author and Finisher of our faith knows where things will end up for us. Our foremothers and forefathers of the faith experienced this same reality.

Adam and Eve's story didn't end as they were driven from Eden. Naomi's didn't end with the death of her husband and sons. Peter's didn't end when he betrayed his Lord, and Mary Magdalene's didn't end as she wept by the tomb. Lazarus didn't stay in the grave. Neither did Jesus. Neither will you. The end of your hopes isn't the end of you; and if you're redeemed, not even your end is *the end*. Not even the death of you will truly be the death of you.

Where Does It End?

A few months ago, I taught a lesson in my women's Bible study. We'd spent weeks dissecting Christian clichés, and that week we'd reached "This, too, shall pass." As with almost all clichés, I'm not a fan. Some things in life will naturally pass—shepherding children through the terrible twos, for instance, or enduring the long, dark days of winter. But for the most part, the timeline of difficult situations is not assured. How long will I have chronic pain? How long will I be infertile? How long will the heathens rage and the people imagine a vain thing?[86] Not all problems are phases, and not all pain is seasonal. In many situations, to say "This, too, shall pass" is to speak to an area where you have no insight.

Moreover, just because a situation will pass doesn't mean its effects will. I'm writing this draft in March of 2020, at the beginning of the American outbreak of the COVID-19 pandemic. I know that while the crisis will pass, it will leave permanent scars. Already, people have lost jobs and livelihoods. Two friends of mine have already lost parents to the virus. Yes, the pandemic will pass, but I have no idea how it will end—for me or for anybody else. It could progress in ways worse than predicted. It may wind up being less of an issue than others feared. Either way, it is a temporary crisis. It will not be the end of me—even if it's the "end" of me. My soul will live on with my Savior and my God, and this world will end only when he says it will end.[87]

And that ending, my friends, is truly a happy one. The ultimate HEA. We know this because God granted the Apostle John a vision of final things.

> Then I saw a new heaven and a new earth, for the first heaven and the first earth had passed away, and the sea was no more. And I saw the holy city, new Jerusalem, coming down out

---

[86] Psalm 2:1, KJV.

[87] I'm revising this section early in June of 2020 during ongoing #BlackLivesMatter protests in the wake of George Floyd's death. I do not know how any of this will end, either.

of heaven from God, prepared as a bride adorned for her husband. And I heard a loud voice from the throne saying, "Behold, the dwelling place of God is with man. He will dwell with them, and they will be his people, and God himself will be with them as their God. He will wipe away every tear from their eyes, and death shall be no more, neither shall there be mourning, nor crying, nor pain anymore, for the former things have passed away." And he who was seated on the throne said, "Behold, I am making all things new." Also he said, "Write this down, for these words are trustworthy and true." And he said to me, "It is done! I am the Alpha and the Omega, the beginning and the end. To the thirsty I will give from the spring of the water of life without payment. The one who conquers will have this heritage, and I will be his God and he will be my son…And I saw no temple in the city, for its temple is the Lord God the Almighty and the Lamb. And the city has no need of sun or moon to shine on it, for the glory of God gives it light, and its lamp is the Lamb. By its light will the nations walk, and the kings of the earth will bring their glory into it, and its gates will never be shut by day—and there will be no night there. They will bring into it the glory and the honor of the nations. But nothing unclean will ever enter it, nor anyone who does what is detestable or false, but only those who are written in the Lamb's book of life.[88]

All things new. God as our light as we live in a kingdom whose gates never shut. What's happening to me now is not the end—it is merely a break in my storyline. It may be the end of a chapter, but it's not the end of the book.[89]

Discussion Questions:

1. In fiction, do you prefer HEA or HFN endings? Why?

_____

_____

_____

2. What is your opinion on the ongoing popularity of HEA? Do you think this is more a case of the markets driving the public imagination or the other way around?

_____

_____

_____

---

[88] Revelation 21:1-7; 22-27.
[89] For this specific wording, I'm indebted to conversations with BJ Thompson.

3. While we know our true HEA begins when King Jesus rules and reigns, what would your current HFN look like? What responsibilities do you bear in seeing it come to pass?

   _____

   _____

   _____

4. Consider this quote: "The end of your hopes isn't the end of you; and if you're redeemed, not even your end is *the end*. Not even the death of you will truly be the death of you." What thoughts and feelings do you have when you read this? Would you offer any counterpoints to this statement?

   _____

   _____

   _____

Notes

_____

_____

_____

_____

_____

_____

_____

_____

_____

_____

_____

_____

_____

_____

_____

_____

_____

_____

_____

_____

_____

_____

_____

Chapter 9

|

As a writer and voracious reader, I spend a lot of my time with my nose planted in books. I also watch some movies and TV. From time to time, people raise sincere questions about matters of conscience in these areas. Questions arise both about the amount of time I invest and the nature of what I consume.

- "That docuseries is *eight hours long*. That's an entire work shift!"

- "You read *that* book? The author's an atheist!" (or "There's witchcraft in it!" or "The message is anti-Christian!")

- "Aren't you worried that pop culture will have a corrupting influence on the way you think?"

- "What are you getting out of all this, anyway?"

We can all agree that the last few chapters speak to what I'm "getting out of it"—and what you can, too. But there are some valid concerns here. I don't read just *any* book. I don't watch *every* movie. Boundaries do need to be established, but I don't believe my boundaries will necessarily be everyone's.

Boundaries

In Scripture, we're told to set our affections on the things above, not on things on this earth.[90] As we've previously discussed, exercising Christian discernment means seeking the good in all we do—including in how we consume media. It isn't so much about what we consume as how it affects us. To the extent that this world's narratives are swaying my affections, I am in danger. To the extent that the Holy Spirit is critiquing and correcting the narratives I'm consuming, I am safe.

There are cases from Scripture to be made that we may exercise our Christian liberty *and* that we must abstain from otherwise permissible elements for the sake of siblings-in-Christ with more tender consciences.[91] That we can rest and enjoy this world, *and* that we should not fritter away our time in lazy and frivolous pursuits.[92] That once we are in Christ, there is no longer any condemnation; that all things are permissible, *and* that not all things are profitable.[93]

My point is this. I refuse to give you a flow chart by which you can determine the exact number of hours you can safely spend reading novels or watching TV. I will not delineate an exact MPAA rating appropriate for Christians. I give no opinion as to whether songs marked *Explicit Content* belong in your music mixes. Instead, I offer a simple solution with complex applications.

---

[90] Colossians 3:2.
[91] 1 Corinthians 8:1-12.
[92] Ecclesiastes 8:15; 9:7; 10:18.
[93] Romans 8:1; 1 Corinthians 6:12.

Spend time meditating on where and how you spend your attention and affections. Ask the Spirit to reveal how your cultural consumption affects you. Are you influenced by the mindset of what you're consuming, or is the Spirit at work in you throughout the process, guiding how you process the messages? Bring your strengths, weaknesses, and spiritual responsibilities before God. By all means, discuss these matters with a mentor or spiritual parent; but ultimately, the Spirit holds you accountable.

Brother James says that pure and undefiled religion includes keeping yourself "unstained" from the world.[94] Not every book, movie, TV, or song lyric with questionable content will necessarily leave an indelible stain on my soul. Think about how stains work. Grape juice in a cup won't necessarily stain my clothes. Unless, of course, I spill it down myself in an effort to guzzle it. It's not the element itself that caused the stain but *the nature of my interaction with it.* When it comes to being stained by the world, so much depends on what's going on in my mind and heart, what my temptations and tendencies are, and the attitude with which I approach what I'm consuming. Yes, there are lines to be drawn—I've never pretended there are not. But the lines aren't universal or easy to place.

In my Fundamentalist school, I was told this meant I should not let "the world" into my heart by watching movies and TV or listening

---

[94] James 1:27. Plus caring for widows and orphans. You can't just sit at home watching Netflix and writing Christian think pieces.

to popular music. I could not read *The Scarlet Letter* because the plot revolved around adultery. Yes, ideas and philosophies flow through the arts. But maturing faith involves a growing ability to analyze what we're consuming. A mind fixed on Christ and nurtured by the Spirit through the Word of God will learn to spot Satan's lies reflected in the culture. It will recognize them as hollow and not feel undue temptation toward participation or perpetuation.

Certainly, a child need not be exposed to mature content (that label exists for a reason), but to hide children completely from society's common stories is more than simply futile. In seeking to do so, you're also shielding children from the very lessons they need to start applying and exercising their faith.

Flexing

Children learn to flex their discernment muscles the same way we learn to flex physical muscles. We start small and work our way up. When I first started at the gym, I was given five-pound free weights because that's all I could handle. The first time my friend Jodee showed me how to deadlift, she only had me lift the bar. Why? I needed to learn the proper technique first. Otherwise, I'd hurt myself.

I couldn't expect to show up at the gym and start deadlifting hundreds of pounds, and we can't expect our children to automatically mature in discerning faith. We can, however, give them gradual opportunities to exercise spiritual discernment. This process isn't as complicated as it sounds. Read a book or watch a movie together. Then talk about it.[95] Give them a chance to seek the good in what they're taking in. What did they like about what they saw? What did they not like? Did anything in the story make them uncomfortable? Did they approve or disapprove of the characters' choices? I like to ask, "What would you have done in that situation? The same thing, or something different?" Then, after they've worked through that, we talk about how the teachings of Scripture could apply to the dilemma.

I'm not a parent and have never raised children, but I've had a long career working with kids in the American school system, teaching writing and literature and working through stories with them. Children are incredibly thoughtful but need guidance to stay on track and work through challenging conversations. Some of the best and most engaging discussions I've had about stories and storytelling have been with kids. If you can possibly find margin in your life to read stories and discuss them with kids, you will not regret it. If nothing else, use the movies and shows they're already watching to frame your discussions. Start small if you must, but start somewhere. It will benefit them and you.

Drawing Lines

There are definitely lines to draw, but we can't teach children how to establish those lines if we haven't worked through the process for ourselves. Neither absolute rejection nor absolute acceptance of

---

[95] Driving in the car from one place to another is a great opportunity for this. Kids are usually bored in the car, and many feel freer to express themselves when you're not staring directly at them while they think.

cultural artifacts is safe. The truth is somewhere in the middle—but where?

The line will not be in the same place for everyone. For example, I can watch a documentary about a serial murderer and not be tempted to kill a string of victims myself. (I promise.) I can read a novel with characters who spout racial slurs and never "slip up" and use such language in real life. Why? These elements aren't drawn out of me because they're not in my heart in the first place. I observe them as an outsider, experiencing no vicarious thrill.

I can't say the same thing for all questionable elements. Sensuality and sexual content both affect me. They speak to an inner lust just waiting to be called out. While I can watch a movie with foul discourse and violence and not feel drawn to join in, sensuality and sexual content tempt me to participate vicariously. In other words, sex scenes stain my soul. I cannot observe and remain unspotted from the world.

Along similar lines, I have to be careful with comedy, particularly stand-up. So many comedians indulge in crass and mean-spirited humor. This is the sort of talk my old nature revels in. The more I watch, the more I enjoy vicarious thrills, and the more I feel prompted to engage the world in a similar way. Stand-up speaks to my natural mean-spiritedness, nurturing it and seeking to draw it out. Hence, I keep a limited diet of stand-up. I cannot in good conscience gorge myself on what stains my soul.

One Caveat

I want to offer one caveat here. In the section above, I've pointed out sexual content and stand-up comedy as two things that stain my soul. I don't pretend they're the only ones, and I don't pretend to know what else could be added to that list.

We're not the best judges of our own hearts. Scripture affirms that the heart is a deceiver.[96] My heart knows what it wants to see, what it wants to soak in. Despite the reality that the blood of Christ has cleansed me from my sin, temptation still operates. Historically, I've been good at justifying my choices to myself. That's why I don't have super settled categories for what I consume. I need check-ins with the Holy Spirit; I must ask him to check me. If there is something that's influencing me, I may not notice it myself—or may not want to notice. I must pray, as the Psalmist David did, "Search me, O God, and know my heart! Try me and know my thoughts! And see if there be any grievous way in me, and lead me in the way everlasting!"[97]

I need this in a special way because so much of my media consumption takes place in solitude. I am not currently married, and I live alone. Most of my reading and watching happens in privacy. Without constant earthly companionship to hold me accountable, I lean even more on the heavenly.

---

[96] Jeremiah 33:3.
[97] Psalm 139:23-34.

I cannot assume that my experiences are normative. We're all different people with divergent personalities, inclinations, and pasts. Personality, generational habits, gender, and culture also play roles here. We're not all the same. You may be able to watch stand-up without descending into mean-spirited mockery. Sensual content might not lead you to lust. Though I find that hard to imagine, I know you don't answer to me for the content you consume. We all answer to God.

Discussion Questions:

1. How much time do you spend in cultural consumption each week? Add it up if you can.

   _____

   _____

   _____

2. How do you decide how much time to invest in these areas? What principles guide these decisions?

   _____

   _____

   _____

3. What elements are dangerous for your soul? Knowing they're an issue for you, do you still willingly engage with them or do you seek to avoid them?

   _____

   _____

   _____

4. How can we exercise discernment and seek the good in what we consume? How can we pass these skills down to the next generation? What value is there in doing so?

———————————————————————

———————————————————————

———————————————————————

Notes

_____

_____

_____

_____

_____

_____

_____

_____

_____

_____

_____

_____

_____

_____

_____

_____

_____

_____

_____

_____

_____

_____

_____

Chapter 10

|

At the outset of this book, I said there was a time when I wouldn't have been able to see Jesus Christ reflected in the culture even if you gave me specific examples. As you can see, that's changed. Rather than fearing cultural artifacts, I've learned to exercise discernment in my cultural intake. I also understand that because culture makers are made in the image of God themselves, the work they produce can reflect timeless and eternal truths whether they realize it or not. But this can only be appreciated by those who have ears to hear and eyes to see.

Much truth is hidden from society. Unless we've grasped the foundational truths of the gospel, other truths may continue to elude us. As the Apostle Paul once pointed out to the church at Corinth, the gospel is veiled to those still on the outside Christ.[98] But the blackout is not complete. The True Light has come. It shines in the darkness, and the darkness cannot overcome it. As John the Baptist did before us, we bear witness to the Light.[99]

Because the light of the gospel has shined on us, we're in a much better position to see this world for what it is, understand our place in it as a Christian, and recognize ourselves as both a product of society and a contributor to it. Are we contributing work that befits our station as

---

[98] 2 Corinthians 4:2-6.
[99] John 1:1-9.

daughters and sons of the Kingdom? This, for the believer, is the essential question. Our beliefs must be expressed in our behavior. An inner, personal belief system is insufficient to reflect our sanctification. Faith without works is dead.[100]

When we connect to the Body of Christ, he links us not just to himself but to one another. Not simply locally, regionally, or nationally. The church of Christ is global. It spans millennia. We are part of the fellowship of the unashamed, a witness passed down through generations. When the gospel goes to work in us, it sparks inner change that leads to collective action. Surrounded by that great cloud of witnesses, sons and daughters of God lock arms and move forward as one. We live, love, and labor within our narrative, waiting for the dawning of our truest Happily Ever After.

We don't know where we are in the timeline. Even with the prophecies of Scripture, we can't predict how long this chapter will last. But we know how the book ends.

So, we read Scripture. We watch and pray. Sing and dance. We tell and re-tell the stories of the saints who have gone before us. We teach them to our children. They teach theirs. We testify to our faith in word and deed. We do justice, love mercy, and walk humbly.[101]

Through it all, we hold fast to this essential truth. By coming embodied to earth, Jesus entered our narrative. By calling us as

---

[100] James 1:22.
[101] Micah 6:8.

daughters and sons, he invites us to enter his. This is the greatest story ever told.

Discussion Questions:

1. In what ways is the gospel hidden to those who don't believe? How might this "hiddenness" change the way unbelieving society engages with their own stories? In what ways will people of faith engage differently?

   _____

   _____

   _____

2. Consider the concluding statement: "This is the greatest story ever told." To what does *this* refer? Do you agree or disagree with that statement?

   _____

   _____

   _____

3. In what specific ways have your thoughts and feelings about cultural artifacts changed as a result of reading this book? Moving forward, will you engage differently with stories and storytelling?

_____

_____

_____

Notes

Acknowledgments

|

To Jesus my King: thank you for saving me. I pray the Spirit continues to teach me the best way to honor the Father and love the brethren as I live out the gospel.

To my beta readers: Hilary Forrest, Laura Hughes, Bethany Buchanan, Sam Won, and Lucy Crabtree. Thank you for pushing back, critiquing, questioning, encouraging, and all-around improving this book. The message is clearer and the communication stronger because of you. May God reward you for your work and labor of love.

Thanks also to Autumn Buchanan and Vicki Olachea. You know what you did.

To Fayelle Ewuake, Marissa Jancovic, Becky L. McCoy, Megan Whitson Lee, and Blake Collier: Thank you for your input regarding horror and faith. You enabled me to construct a helpful section without having to traumatize myself.

To my church family and blood family: I can't imagine writing without the support of a community. Thank you for pouring love and truth into my life. Your ministry is seen, known, and remembered by God. Mom, you taught me how to read and instilled in me a love for learning that has never been quenched. Dad, you taught us Scripture and how to change a tire. We honor you both. To everyone who dropped off food (meal kits! soup!) and toilet paper (#pandemic) and asked how the writing was going: I love you. Keep up the good work.

To everyone who made it all the way through this book: You deserve your own special word. Thank you for taking time to read this. May its message make a difference.

About the Author

Ruth Buchanan is a Christian writer who holds degrees in ministry and theology. She's traditionally published in the areas of fiction, non-fiction, plays, and sacred scripts. Though usually clamped to the keyboard, Ruth is also an eager reader, an enthusiastic traveler, and the world's most reluctant runner. She serves as Director of Literary Services for *Build a Better Us*.

. . .

Connect with Ruth on Social Media

Twitter: @RuthMBuchanan | Instagram: @RuthMBuchanan

www. RuthBuchananAuthor.com

Connect with Build a Better Us

Facebook: facebook.com/bbusocial/ | Twitter: @buildabtetterus

Instagram: @bbusocial

www.buildabetterus.com

WHAT TO READ NEXT
AVAILABLE NOW!

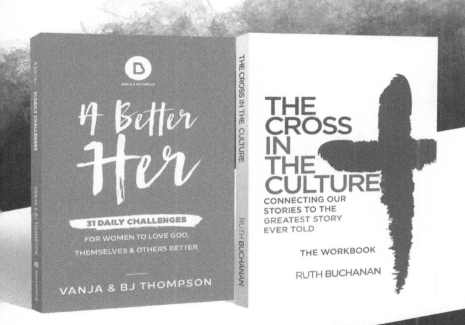

WWW.RUTHBUCHANANAUTHOR.COM

CPSIA information can be obtained
at www.ICGtesting.com
Printed in the USA
LVHW091020201020
669268LV00007B/419